THE GOLDEN LAND

The Story of Jewish Immigration to America

Experience the Achievements of American Jews through Removable Documents and Artifacts

RABBI JOSEPH TELUSHKIN

Harmony Books  New York

For my cherished mother, Helen Telushkin, a lover of the three things this book is about—Jews, America, and history.

Published by Harmony Books, New York, New York.
Member of the Crown Publishing Group

Random House, Inc. New York, Toronto, London, Sydney, Auckland
www.randomhouse.com

Harmony Books is a registered trademark and the Harmony Books colophon is a trademark of Random House, Inc.

The Golden Land: The Story of Jewish Immigration to America is produced by becker&mayer!, Bellevue, Washington.
www.beckermayer.com

Edited by Dale Cotton and Ben Raker
Designed by Katie LeClercq
Production management by Cindy Curren
Research by Adrienne Wiley and Shayna Ian
Additional research and translations by Ari Kinsberg

Printed and assembled in Singapore

Library of Congress Cataloging-in-Publication Data

Telushkin, Rabbi Joseph, 1948–
    The golden land : the story of Jewish immigration to America : experience the achievements of American Jews through removable documents and artifacts / Rabbi Joseph Telushkin.
    Includes bibliographical references (p.).
    1. Jews—History—United States. 2. Jews—Migrations—History. 3. United
States—Emigration and immigration. 4. Europe—Emigration and immigration. 5.
Immigrants—United States—History. 6. United States—Ethnic relations. I. Title: the story
of Jewish immigration to America. II. Title.

E184.35 .T45 2002
305.8924073—dc21

                                                                2001039888

ISBN 0-609-60904-1
10 9 8 7 6 5 4 3 2 1
First Edition

CONTENTS

1492
JEWRY'S DARKEST DAWN

It is a long-held rabbinic notion that at the time of greatest catastrophe, God's deliverance is already being prepared. This teaching applies to two events that occurred within a span of three days in the summer of 1492. On July 31st, King Ferdinand and Queen Isabella, acting at the instigation of the Spanish Inquisition, expelled Spain's 200,000-strong Jewish community. Only Jews who converted to Christianity were permitted to remain.

During their Golden Age, when Jews had been invited to hold high government positions, Jewish religious and cultural life flourished. Following the 1492 edict, Spanish Jews fled by ship to Portugal (from which they were expelled five years later), Holland, Turkey, Morocco, and elsewhere. Many drowned while trying to reach safety. In some cases, Spanish ship captains charged Jewish passengers enormous sums, then threw them overboard in the middle of the ocean. Some of these thieves, who had heard rumors that the fleeing Jews had swallowed gold and diamonds, stabbed them to death, then ripped open their stomachs hoping to find treasures.

Some Spanish Jews pretended to convert to Christianity and continued to live secretly as Jews. Known as *Marranos*, they kept their identities hidden from all except immediate family members and others whom they knew shared their convictions. To be exposed as a Marrano meant being subjected to the most brutal forms of torture, and possible execution, at the hands of the Inquisition.

On August 3, 1492, three days after the Jews' expulsion, Christopher Columbus and his fleet of three ships—the *Niña*, *Pinta*, and *Santa Maria*—set sail for India on a voyage that instead brought him and his crew to North America. Of the ninety sailors on his ships, historians have identified five as Marranos. They likely sailed with Columbus in the hope of finding a society more hospitable to Jews than was Spain. One, Luis de Torres, a man who knew Hebrew and Arabic and who served as the ship's interpreter, was the first member of Columbus's crew to set foot on North American soil (in what is now Cuba).

Thus, at the very moment of the most disastrous event of medieval Jewish history, the expulsion of Spanish Jewry, the voyage began that would end with the European discovery of the land that would become the United States. This new country would come to house the largest, most prosperous, and most successful Jewish community in diaspora history. As the rabbis so long ago taught, on the day of catastrophe, salvation already is being prepared.

The Golden Land tells the story of the migrations that have created what is today an American-Jewish community of six million people, migrations that have shaped the Jews and that have, in turn, deeply influenced America. America has been unique in Jewish life. For the first time in our history, we are living in a place in which we have been regarded as citizens from the country's very beginning. Jews have been able to participate in virtually every aspect of the society. Indeed, the successive waves of migration that brought Jews to America have transformed both Jewish and American history. How they have done so is the story to which we will now turn.

Opposite page: *Hearing of the impending exile of the Jews, it is said that a group of Jewish men knelt before King Ferdinand and Queen Isabella of Spain, offering to buy an end to the Inquisition with 30,000 ducats. This offer tempted the royal figures, but the influential Grand Inquisitor Torquemada (shown holding a crucifix) prevailed upon them to pass the edict that expelled Jews from Spain in 1492.*

Top: *Born a Marrano Jew in Portugal, Isaac Aboab da Fonseca (1605–1693) immigrated to the free Dutch colony in Recife, Brazil and became the first rabbi in the New World.*

Bottom: *Many Jews burned at the stake during the autos-da-fé (public executions of heretics) that were hallmarks of the Inquisition.*

THE FIRST COMMUNITY

The first group of openly Jewish settlers arrived in North America in 1654. The ship *Ste. Catherine* deposited them at the small Dutch settlement of New Amsterdam (which was captured in 1664 by the British and renamed New York). The group consisted of six families totaling twenty-three people, including thirteen children and two widows.

To this day, American Jewry is largely identified with Jews whose ancestors came from Germany in the 1800s and during the 1930s, and from eastern Europe in the late nineteenth and early twentieth centuries. This very first group, however, was composed of Jews fleeing from Recife, a Brazilian city ruled by the Dutch that had just been conquered by Portugal. The city's 650 Jews knew the arrival of the Portuguese army would soon be followed by the arrival of the Portuguese Inquisition, which was committed to persecuting the Jews and expelling them from territories it controlled.

As a result, almost all of Recife's Jews returned to Holland, their country of origin and a society that granted the Jews if not full equality, then more rights than did any other country in Europe. But this small group, about whom little information exists, apparently was poor. Having no prospects to return to in Holland, they set sail, intending to reach the islands of the Caribbean. Their ship made port in Jamaica, then Cuba, but the Spanish did not allow them to remain, and they were forced to pay an outrageous amount for a captain to take them on to New Amsterdam.

Peter Stuyvesant, the governor of New Amsterdam, quickly sent a letter to his employer in Amsterdam, the Dutch West India Company, requesting permission to expel the Jews who had arrived, claiming that they were poor and would become a public charge. In addition, if Jews started working in New Amsterdam, their characteristic commercial activities—"usury and deceitful trading with the Christians"—would harm the community. In short, the Jews "were very repugnant." Stuyvesant proposed, therefore, "that the deceitful race—such hateful enemies and blasphemers of the name of Christ—be not allowed further to infect and trouble this new colony."[1]

It was a rare piece of luck for this band of wanderers that Dutch Jews were among the Dutch West India Company's investors, and thereby exerted influence on company policies. The Jewish investors in Amsterdam argued vigorously that their coreligionists be permitted to settle in New Amsterdam, and the pressure worked, up to a point. The Jews could remain in New Amsterdam, "provided the poor among them shall not become a burden to the company or to the community, but be supported by their own nation."[2]

Stuyvesant, however, was allowed to impose other far-reaching restrictions on the Jews. He forbade them to own land or houses, open retail stores, trade with Native Americans, or conduct public prayer services. But despite his malevolent intentions, further pressure exerted by Holland's Jews and reinforced by the Jews in New Amsterdam effectively canceled these restrictions within three years.

In the century after the British wrested control of New Amsterdam from Holland, Jews gradually gained full civil rights within the city. New York became the first society in modern times in which Jews could vote, hold political office, and serve on juries. As historian Deborah Dash Moore concludes: "New York Jews thus obtained political equality before Western European nations began to debate Jewish emancipation."[3]

Nothing displays the improved status of America's Jews better than the letter sent in the late summer of 1790 by newly elected president George Washington to the Jewish community of Newport, Rhode Island (the Touro Congregation). Responding to the message of congratulations the congregation had sent him upon his election, Washington assured the Jewish community that in America Jews would always enjoy equal rights. He wrote, "May the Children of the Stock of Abraham, who dwell in this land, continue to merit and enjoy the good will of the other inhabitants, while everyone shall sit in safety under his own vine and figtree, and there shall be none to make him afraid."

(See page 30 for a transcription of this letter.)

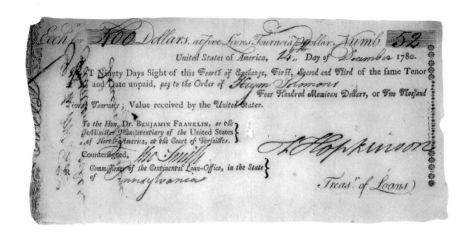

HAYM SALOMON

The Jewish community, in what were now the British colonies, grew slowly. At the time of the American Revolution, there were only an estimated 2,000 to 2,500 Jews scattered throughout the colonies, among a total population of about 2.5 million. Most of them identified, often strongly, with the Revolutionary cause. Historian Richard B. Morris, a careful student of the Revolutionary period, writes that "the roster of American Jewish participants on the side of the Revolution is so impressive that it is clear that Whiggish Jews [meaning Jews who supported the Revolution] constituted an overwhelming majority of the scattered Jewish communities in the thirteen colonies."[4]

Support for the Revolution came first from Jewish businessmen who, like their non-Jewish counterparts, bristled at Britain's restrictive fiscal policies and "taxation without representation." However, the willingness of many Jews to risk their lives in the colonial army suggests that Jewish support for the Revolution did not emanate from economic motives alone; rather, Jews identified with the cause of liberty. Governor James Wright of Georgia, a British loyalist, advocated that Jews be prevented from immigrating to the colony: "For these people . . . were found to a man to have been violent rebels."[5]

Indeed, more Jews were involved in the Revolution than one might expect from the small number in America at that time. The Continental army included Jewish colonels and lieutenant colonels. One outfit in South Carolina became known as the "Jew company" because thirty of its members, half the entire company, were Jewish.

In Philadelphia, Jonas Phillips, a blockade-runner who commandeered supplies from enemy ships, maintained secret wish lists of those supplies in Yiddish. His plan didn't work: When the British seized one of his ships and saw the strange, foreign lettering, they concluded it was a code and impounded the vessel.

With the establishment of the United States as a fully independent country, and the passage of the Constitution in 1788, Jews now lived, for the first time since the destruction of their state some two thousand years earlier, in a country (not just a state, as had been the case with New York) that granted them equal rights. The Jewish community particularly rejoiced at the provision in Article VI that "no religious test shall ever be required as a qualification to any office or public trust under the United States" and at the First Amendment in the Bill of Rights, which forbade Congress from passing any law either respecting an establishment of religion or prohibiting its free exercise. At the gathering held in Philadelphia to celebrate the Constitution's ratification, a special kosher table was provided for Jewish celebrants. And though some states still practiced discrimination (only in 1826, for example, were Maryland's Jews finally permitted to hold public office without submitting to a Christian oath), the standing of Jews in America continued to rise over the coming decades.

Jews Side with Revolutionary Cause

The most famous Jew to serve the Revolutionary cause was the Polish-born Haym Salomon, who arranged the sale of hundreds of thousands of dollars of bonds issued by the new government to raise funds. Some bonds ended up in the Paris and Frankfurt bourses and helped to establish the stability of American credit on European bond markets. As chief bill broker to Robert Morris, the superintendent of finance, Salomon helped make funds available for the expedition against Cornwallis, the campaign that brought the Revolutionary War to a successful end. By extending interest-free loans to Thomas Jefferson, James Madison, and James Monroe—helping these heroes of the Revolution to meet personal expenses— Salomon also made a mockery of Stuyvesant's hateful comment about Jews becoming usurers.

In 1820, 3,000 Jews lived in the United States. By the time of the Civil War their numbers had grown to 150,000; and by 1880 they had reached 250,000, an increase of more than eighty times in just sixty years. This period is known to American-Jewish historians as the era of the great German migration, though the Jews who came during this time were not only from Germany but also from other areas of Europe whose people spoke German or were influenced by German culture (such as Bohemia and Moravia, in what is now the Czech Republic).

The reason for this migration was a combination of antisemitism and the lack of economic opportunities. As rejecters of Jesus and Christianity, Jews were perceived as untrustworthy, even as allies of the Devil. In Germany, antisemitism was magnified by the legacy and teachings of Martin Luther (1483–1546), the father of German nationalism. Remembered today as the founder of Protestantism and a rebel against the Vatican, in his later years Luther evolved into a ferocious antisemite; he wrote of Jews as "an unsufferable, devilish burden" and advocated, among other things, burning all synagogues and forcing Jews to do physical labor.[1]

During Napoleon's rule in the early 1800s, Jewish life in Germany improved significantly. In the areas he conquered, the French emperor extended to Jews the equal rights accorded to French Jewry since shortly after the French Revolution. With Napoleon's defeat in 1815, a nationalist reaction set in and Jews were subjected to antisemitic laws and even physical attacks.

Some converted to Christianity to evade the antisemitic laws, but most refused to do so and soon found antisemitic pressures growing. In 1819 students at the University of Würzburg led an attack against the local Jewish community. As they pillaged the Jewish area and beat up Jews, the students chanted, "Hep, hep!," an antisemitic chant dating back to the Crusades ("Hep" stood for the Latin words *Hiersolyma Est Perdita*, "Jerusalem is destroyed"). This battle cry of the rioters inspired the Hep! Hep! movement, whose leaders went on to organize attacks against other Jewish communities throughout Germany. About the same time, a delegate in the Bavarian Diet, aware that the United States was one of the few Western societies that permitted unrestricted immigration, declared: "The Jews must clear out and go to America." To make matters worse, in much of Germany an old quota was reimposed that limited the number of Jews in any city who were permitted to marry and start families, a cruel attempt to keep the Jewish population from growing.

New York City was the immigrants' most frequently sought destination—by mid-century, sixteen thousand Jews lived there—but an increasing number of Jews started heading elsewhere. By 1850 six thousand lived in Philadelphia and four thousand in Baltimore, and ten years later, Cincinnati hosted a Jewish community of almost ten thousand.[2] The new immigrants were willing to move wherever economic opportunities presented themselves. Thus Jewish communities soon sprang up in such cities as Louisville, Minneapolis, Rochester, and Columbus.

Restricted from many professions and discriminated against in well-established business enterprises, Jews focused their entrepreneurial energy in specific fields. They also arrived both poor and generally without much education, so it is perhaps not surprising that such a high percentage turned to peddling. In fact, by 1860 the majority of peddlers in the U.S.

Prayers Across the Ocean

This prayer book, printed small for travel, belonged to a woman who crossed the Atlantic in 1875, toward the end of the major exodus of Jews from Germany. The Hebrew title reads: "Daily Prayer Book (*Tefilla Mikol Hashana*) Small Offering for Travelers and Sea Farers to America (God Bless It). A Miniature Edition of Fine Beautiful Print." (See page 30 for further explanation.) The book has a Hebrew inscription that shows the depth of feeling behind this traveler's gift:

To my beloved

Small is my offering.
Let it not be compared to my love.
Please know that it comes from me:
a sign of love for thee
from Moses Margolioth.
28 May 1875

were Jewish.[3] While peddling could be profitable, it was difficult and often dangerous work. The merchandise on a peddler's back—notions, dry goods, spices, old clothes—frequently weighed a hundred or more pounds, and it was common for a peddler to walk ten to fifteen miles a day. Peddlers were subject to attacks by fierce dogs, and their merchandise was a constant lure to thieves; records show that peddlers were sometimes ambushed and killed by highwaymen.

What is perhaps most remarkable is the speed with which some peddlers went from carrying merchandise on their backs to establishing stores and, eventually, retail empires. Others reinvested the small stakes they earned from peddling to make fortunes as bankers and, by the time of the Civil War, international financiers.

Marcus Goldman, the future founder of Goldman, Sachs and Co., arrived in Philadelphia in 1848, and peddled there for two years before opening a men's clothing store. Samuel Rosenwald peddled on foot in the South, finally acquired a horse and wagon, then moved to Springfield, Illinois, to open a store. A generation later, his son Julius purchased a small watch company called Sears, Roebuck and subsequently built it into the world's largest mail-order house. German-Jewish immigrants whose names are recognizable because of the stores they created include Altman, Bloomingdale, Filene, Gimbel, and Saks.

The German-Jewish migration also had a profound effect on the social and religious character of American-Jewish life. In 1820, just before the migration began, a total of eight congregations served the entire American-Jewish community; by 1880 there were close to three hundred. German immigrants founded the B'nai B'rith society in 1843, a social and cultural organization which in the ensuing century established the Anti-Defamation League to combat prejudice and discrimination (1913) and the Hillel movement to service the social and religious needs of Jewish college students (1923).

German Jews also established the Reform movement in this country, today the largest denomination among American Jews. In 1875, under the leadership of Rabbi Isaac Mayer Wise, the Hebrew Union College (HUC) was established in Cincinnati to advance the principles of Reform Judaism. In 1886 other German Jews, angered at the far-reaching changes in Jewish tradition the early Reform movement had introduced—for example, dropping the Jewish dietary laws and the belief that the Jews were a people as well as a religion—played a major role in establishing the Jewish Theological Seminary (JTS) in New York. The JTS offered a traditional view of Jewish teachings and became the flagship institution for what became known as Conservative Judaism.

Despite the hardships of poverty, discrimination, and lack of education, German Jews contributed significantly to cultural and religious life. The retail stores, international banking institutions, and newly formed religious movements provided a strong footing for all Jewish immigrants, while changing the shape of nineteenth-century American cities in the process.

JOSEPH SELIGMAN

From Peddler to Banker

In a class by himself among the nineteenth-century Jewish immigrants was the banker Joseph Seligman. After arriving in 1837 and peddling for two years in Pennsylvania, he accumulated $500. He used some of this money to bring over two of his seven brothers, who also became peddlers, then opened a store in Lancaster, Pennsylvania. Within a few years, the eight brothers, all of whom had immigrated, opened stores in many parts of the country. By the early 1850s Joseph had sent two brothers to San Francisco, from where he started importing vast quantities of gold to New York. During the Civil War, Seligman obtained clothing contracts for army uniforms that the government, which was short on cash, paid off with negotiable credit notes. He soon learned that to convert these notes into cash, they had to be sold on the open market. By 1864 this one family had marketed over half of the $250,000,000 of Union bonds sold abroad in Europe, thus playing a crucial role in gaining deeply needed financial and diplomatic backing for the Union.

Above: One of the first of the estimated 1,500 Jews killed in the Proskurov pogrom, this victim joined the tens of thousands of Russian Jews killed in pogroms in the forty years following Czar Alexander II's assassination. Thousands of Jews fled to America to escape this devastation.

The Great Migration

1881–1923
THE JEWS OF EASTERN EUROPE

The first great exodus in Jewish history, the journey of the former Israelite slaves from Egyptian slavery to freedom in Canaan, occurred over a 40-year period and included, according to the biblical account, some two million men, women, and children.

Another vast migration occurred 3,200 years later, also over a period of about 40 years (1881–1923), and also involving about two million people. But instead of heading for the Promised Land of Israel, these Jews from Russia, Romania, and Austria-Hungary made their way from eastern and central Europe to the United States. About 7 percent of the eastern European Jews went to western Europe, and 10 to 13 percent went to Canada, Argentina, South Africa, Australia, or Palestine (from these last ranks came the pioneers of the First and Second *Aliyah*—waves of immigration to the land of Israel). The rest, 80 percent, came to the United States.[1]

The overwhelming majority of these immigrants came from Russia. The immediate cause for their migration was the 1881 pogroms (government-sponsored riots against the Jewish community, accompanied by murder and pillage). That March, a band of young revolutionaries engineered the assassination of Czar Alexander II. His predecessor, Nicholas I, drafted Jewish boys twelve years old and younger for twenty-five-year service in the czarist army, where few, if any, could advance to officer status. Jewish soldiers were continually pressured to convert to Russian Orthodoxy. Alexander, Nicholas's successor, had a kinder nature; it was he who liberated the serfs in 1861. Upon Alexander's assassination, however, the Jews again became targets and victims. In the year following the assassination, pogroms were carried out in 225 communities. In December 1881, a massive antisemitic riot took place in Warsaw, then under Russian rule. Synagogues were sacked and 1,500 Jewish homes and stores were destroyed before Russian troops finally stopped the rioting.

The government's strategy was obvious: Focus peasant discontent away from the czar and nobles by depicting the Jews (many of whom, as small-businessmen, were in frequent contact with the peasants) as the oppressors and enemies of the lower classes. Unfortunately, Jews were natural targets. In the fiercely Russian Orthodox society of nineteenth-century Russia, Jews were still widely perceived as Christ-killers. Even into the twentieth century, the czarist government prosecuted Jews on accusations of murdering Christian children to use their blood in religious rituals.

In 1882 the new regime of Alexander III declared the May Laws, which prohibited Jews from living in villages (five hundred thousand Jews were soon expelled from rural areas) and from purchasing or renting land. A few years later, Konstantin Pobedonostev, head of the Russian Orthodox Church and a strong influence on the czar, clarified the government's goals in a statement that made Russian Jews' blood run cold: "One-third [of the Jews] should emigrate, one-third become Christianized, and one-third should perish."[2]

The flight that Pobedonostev so desired had already begun with the pogroms: 13,000 Jews left Russia for the United States, almost as many as the 15,000 who had migrated in the preceding decade. Between 1881 and 1890, a total of 240,000 Jews emigrated from Russia

to the United States, with profound effects on American-Jewish life, especially in New York City. In 1881, on the eve of this great migration, 80,000 Jews lived there. By 1901 the city's Jewish population had swelled to 510,000. Nine years later, the two-square-mile area of Manhattan's Lower East Side housed 542,000 Jews, making it the most densely populated area in the world at that time.

The Jews who left Russia, however, were not just fleeing antisemitism; terrible poverty drove them as well. Indeed, the more affluent Jews tended to remain in their homeland, as did the most religiously observant. The rabbinic leadership, having heard frightening reports of irreligiosity in America (where it was common, for example, for laborers to work on the Sabbath), urged Jews not to risk their souls in the country rabbis commonly referred to as the *treife medina* (the "unkosher land"). At a time when between 5 and 10 percent of the Jews in eastern Europe worked in the professions, only 50 of the 150,000 east European Jews who migrated to the United States in 1906 listed themselves as professionals.[3] The overwhelming majority were manual laborers, 60 percent working in the clothing industry.

The immigrants' great poverty made their passage to America difficult to attain. A ticket between Hamburg and New York cost $34, more than many Jews earned in a year, and for that sum one traveled in the dreaded class known as "steerage." On one typical German ship, the *Amerika*, two thousand passengers were crowded into three decks; they were provided with double-decker iron beds and straw mattresses with no pillows during the two-week voyage. The passengers washed themselves with cold seawater, without benefit of soap or towels. The shipping lines provided no dining area or public rooms for steerage passengers, because they didn't want to waste space into which additional passengers could be crowded. Low partitions between the beds allowed for little, if any, privacy. A journalist accompanying the passengers reported that the food consisted largely of "the hash of grisly beef and warm potatoes that would not have been tolerated in the poorest restaurant."[4] On many ships, the toilets were open troughs that were rarely cleaned. In immigrants' memoirs, one repeatedly comes across tales of terrible seasickness caused not just by the rocking of the boat, but also by the filth and foul smell of the surroundings.

For the large majority of Jews who arrived after 1892, the port of entry into America was Ellis Island, a tiny islet between Manhattan and Staten Island, which was soon to handle as many as seven thousand immigrants in a day. While it was remembered fondly by some immigrants, Ellis Island was also the scene of many pitiful tragedies. All incoming immigrants were examined by physicians; those found to have certain eye disorders, such as trachoma, or "contagious and loathsome" diseases, such as tuberculosis, were sent back to Europe, at the shipping company's expense. Once a family member was declared "diseased," the rest of the family faced the agonizing decision of whether to return to Europe or to send the sick person back alone. However, even if they wished to go back with their sick relative, most arriving immigrants lacked the funds to do so.

Travel Routes

"Jews from the Ukraine and southern Russia crossed the Austro-Hungarian border illegally, often to Brody, traveled from there by train to Warsaw or Berlin, and regrouped to go to Hamburg, Rotterdam, Amsterdam, and Antwerp where for $34 . . . one could purchase a steamship ticket to the New World. Jews from western Russia came surreptitiously across the borders, while the Austro-Hungarians could cross legally. And the Romanians arrived at the northern ports mainly through Vienna."[5]

Left: The Educational Alliance, sponsor of many programs to help immigrants in America, reinforced children's identification with their new country through such events as Americanization Day, shown here in 1910.

Below: Children orphaned by Russian pogroms wait at Ellis Island in 1908. These orphans depended on relatives and aid organizations to provide new homes for them in America.

Happily, the large majority of immigrants, Jews and non-Jews alike, made it through Ellis Island and were admitted to the United States. For most Jews, their first destination was Manhattan's Lower East Side. Though it is now well over a century since Jews first flocked to this area, the neighborhood's street names—Canal, Hester, Rivington, Essex, and others—still ring in the ears of tens of thousands of grandchildren and great grandchildren of these immigrants. To this day, the scenes from the Lower East Side dominate Jewish recollections of their early immigrant experiences. The writer Maurice Hindus, then fresh from rural Russia, recalled that "several blocks from where we lived was roaring, bustling Hester Street. The pavement was lined with stalls and pushcarts, and men with . . . baskets suspended on leather straps from their necks pushed their way along, crying their wares—needles, thread, shoelaces, soap, socks—like hawkers in a Russian bazaar."[6]

By 1914 the Lower East Side, concentrated on a little over 1 percent of New York's total land area, housed a sixth of the city's total population, and the area's population exceeded that of Detroit. Most immigrants lived in "dumbbell" tenement buildings. Commonly six stories tall, the buildings were shaped like dumbbells, four apartments to a floor, two at each end of a narrow separating corridor. Only one of the four rooms in each tiny apartment received direct light from the street in front or the yard in back. Residents shared a common toilet in the hallway. A man writing to *The Jewish Daily Forward* (often referred to as *The Forward*) letter section described his life as a janitor on Stanton Street, "where the sun is ashamed to shine."[7] Not surprisingly, residents of such dwellings tried to spend as little time in them as possible. Children often ran off to swim in the East River.

Because children were usually the only fluent English-speakers in their families, they often had to assume adult responsibilities. Harry Golden remembers that "On the Lower East Side, our parents spoke to us in Yiddish and we answered in English. As a result, a proverb circulated the ghetto: 'In America, the children bring up the parents.'"[8]

Yiddish Theater: *Theatrical depictions of* shtetl *(small Jewish towns in eastern Europe) life gave Yiddish-speaking Jews a place to feel more at home in their New World. By 1918 there were some twenty Yiddish theaters in New York City.*

Journalist Lincoln Steffens, who wrote about the Jewish ghetto in the 1890s with great sympathy, wrote of "one girl of eleven [who] habitually signs the checks and does all the writing necessary in transactions with certain charitable bureaus that help her mother, and during her mother's illness undertook the cooking, washing, and general superintendence of five younger children, one of whom was an infant. . . . Another little girl is the real, although her mother is the ostensible, janitress of a big tenement house, the child conducting all the interviews with Board of Health officials, the street cleaners and other authorities, and personally conducting interviews regarding the renting of rooms, collecting [rent], etc."[9]

As the number of eastern European Jewish immigrants escalated sharply in the early 1900s, many of America's German-Jewish leaders, along with some Jews who had recently come from eastern Europe, concluded that the newcomers should be encouraged to move to less populated parts of the United States. The New York job market was overcrowded, and these "native" Jews feared that the new immigrants would either become unemployed or work for cheap wages, causing other workers to become unemployed. The latter concern in particular set off fears that the new Jewish migration might lead to antisemitism.

In 1907 Jacob Schiff, the greatest Jewish philanthropist of the time, formulated a plan to encourage Jews to migrate to the port city of Galveston, Texas, and head from there to the American South, Midwest, and West. Schiff calculated that a fund of half a million dollars (a very large sum at the time) would be sufficient to direct up to twenty-five thousand Jews to Galveston. His plan took into account all relevant factors save one: few Russian Jews had any desire to live in Galveston or its environs. For Russian Jews, going to America meant going to New York or one of the other major cities on the East Coast, where they could find a welcoming Jewish population; during the eight years that Schiff promoted his plan, a total of only some ten thousand Jews went to Galveston.

Most Jews, therefore, remained on the East Coast, but so hard were these early years for many immigrants that the Yiddish language, already famous in Europe for its large variety of curses (e.g., "May all your teeth fall out except one, and that should ache you"), coined a new one: *a klug tzu Columbus*, "a curse on Columbus" (for having discovered America).

But such curses were meant to be more ironic than serious; they were simply a way of letting off steam. For what was most striking about America to these immigrants was the freedom offered: "I used to marvel how freely I could walk about," one newcomer wrote. "No policeman . . . stops me and brusquely demands to see my passport. . . . Jews speak whatever language they please in public, they wear whatever clothes they wish."[10]

Indeed, with all their complaints about the harsh poverty and difficult work conditions, no other immigrant group embraced America with such enthusiasm. Between 1908 and 1924, 95 percent of Jewish immigrants remained in the United States, at a time when the rate among all other immigrants was only 67 percent. Unlike these other immigrant groups, Russian Jews had little love for the country they had left. Italian and Greek Americans might have sung longing, tuneful songs about their native lands, but how could Russian Jews, whose leaders sponsored pogroms that its citizens carried out, romanticize their native country? The Jews were here to stay, their needs met.

From Enmity to Acceptance
GERMAN JEWS V. RUSSIAN JEWS

The arrival of ever-growing numbers of Russian Jews in the United States triggered alarm and sometimes even anger among many of their German-Jewish co-religionists. Because the large majority of newcomers were poor and uneducated, German Jews worried that the presence of these "primitive people" would inspire antisemitism. Augustus Levey, secretary of the Hebrew Emigrant Aid Society (HEAS, later HIAS, Hebrew Immigrant Aid Society), commented: "A lowering of the opinion in which American Israelites are held . . . can result from the continued residence among us . . . of these wretches."[1]

If that is how sympathetic observers regarded the Russian Jews, one can imagine the feelings of less friendly souls. Isaac Mayer Wise, the most prominent Reform rabbi of the nineteenth century, urged all east European Jews "who do not possess a useful trade [to] stay in Europe. We have enough beggars and humbug-seeking vagabonds here." San Francisco rabbi Jacob Voorsanger's advice was more extreme: simply stop all Jewish immigration to the United States.[2]

Even German-Jewish philanthropic organizations, which did so much to help the arriving immigrants, were often tainted with prejudice. German Jews established Mount Sinai, the former "Jews' Hospital," to provide care for Jewish patients who were often unable to observe Jewish law and custom in non-Jewish hospitals. By the 1880s, the hospital was treating almost 90 percent of its patients—of whom many were east European immigrants—without charge, but house physicians were almost exclusively German Jews.

Fortunately, there were exceptions to this widespread intolerance. In Detroit, the prominent Reform rabbi Leo Franklin urged his congregants and the whole German-Jewish community to embrace the new immigrants, if in somewhat condescending terms: "Oppression has temporarily taken the manhood out of the Russian Jew, yet he is our brother . . . . How dare we expect the world to look with unprejudiced eyes upon us so long as Jew stands against Jew?" Most important, although many German Jews held east European Jews in contempt and feared their presence would stimulate antisemitism, they still recognized their obligation to these immigrants as fellow Jews. Thus, German Jews established such institutions as the Educational Alliance, which sponsored social and educational programs to help educate and "Americanize" the immigrants, and the United Hebrew Charities, to support the poor.

The most significant German-Jewish leader to help reverse hostilities toward eastern European Jews was the investment banker Jacob Schiff (himself an immigrant from Frankfurt, Germany). Schiff not only wrote checks for these new arrivals, but he also took a personal interest in them. On one occasion, when he learned of the presence of a talented sculptor, Julius Butensky, among the new immigrants, he personally went down to the East Fourteenth Street tenement where Butensky lived, only to learn that the artist had been evicted. When Schiff finally located him a week later, he paid Butensky to do a statue of the prophet Isaiah beating his sword into a plowshare. The statue was later exhibited at the Metropolitan Museum of Art.

Left: *Russian Jews in New York City celebrated the Jewish New Year in 1907 at this Lower East Side synagogue. This tiny house of worship was quite different from the uptown synagogues German Jews used.*

Emma Lazarus's "The New Colossus"

Right: Shaken by having witnessed the hordes of humiliated eastern European Jews arriving destitute in her city, Lazarus, a Jew born in New York City, wrote her most famous poem as a tribute. The poem was inscribed at the base of the Statue of Liberty. Though highly sympathetic to refugees of all backgrounds, Lazarus described them as "the wretched refuse of your teeming shores." Of course, in nonpoetic spoken English, "wretched refuse" sounds like a euphemism for "garbage," which sums up the way they were initially viewed.

At a time when many German-Jewish leaders reacted timidly to antisemitism, believing that it was most prudent to ignore such incidents, Schiff, a man seemingly without fear, fought back. When President Taft told Schiff and a delegation of other Jewish leaders, in a 1910 White House meeting, that he wouldn't cancel the 1832 Russo-American commercial treaty—despite the czarist government's refusal to relent in its decades-old policy of not permitting American Jews to obtain visas to Russia—Schiff lashed out at Taft for valuing economic gain above human rights. At the meeting's end, he refused to shake the president's hand. Within a year, a campaign orchestrated by Schiff brought an end to the treaty.[3]

However, the battle that brought Schiff particular renown among the Russian Jews was the one he waged against the Russian government itself. In response to its promotion of antisemitic legislation and pogroms (some six hundred during the years 1903–1906 alone), he proclaimed: "If Czar Alexander II, with one stroke of a pen, could free millions of serfs, who had certainly not attained to the cultural levels of the Jews in Russia, there should be no difficulty in giving the Jews the same civic rights as are accorded to other Russian citizens."[4]

In 1905 the Russo-Japanese War afforded Schiff a concrete opportunity to express his anti-Russian sentiments. He single-handedly arranged a $200,000,000 loan for the Japanese government, which it used to strengthen its army, eventually inflicting a surprising defeat on the Russians. As Russia's Minister of Finance commented: "He [Schiff] alone made it possible for Japan to secure a loan in America." But Schiff did much more than just fight antisemitism. My mother, who grew up on the Lower East Side in the 1920s, still recalls the small trucks that would come around on his instructions to sell immigrant Jews, most of whom were poor, small bottles of milk for a penny.

Also working on behalf of all American Jews were such men as Rabbi Judah Magnes, who created a *kehilla* in New York City, a Jewish communal organization that sought to unite the city's Jews, and Louis Marshall, Magnes's brother-in-law and president of the American Jewish Committee, who emerged as the most powerful Jewish leader of his age. As Ande Manners commented in her book *Poor Cousins*: "In the early years of the twentieth century, Schiff and Marshall went together in the thoughts of their east European co-religionists like lox and bagels."[5]

By the mid-twentieth century, the quarrels between the German-Jewish and the eastern European–Jewish communities had ended. Jews of German and Russian and Polish ancestry married one another, worked together, and shared in the running of national Jewish organizations. Some old-line German-Jewish elitists might have resented such mixing, but Jacob Schiff would have been pleased. Shortly before World War I, while touting the virtues of the eastern European immigrants, he predicted that in no more than half a century the mixture of the German and Russian Jews would be "destined to produce the finest type of Jew of all time."[6]

Emma Lazarus's Handwritten Poem
(See page 31 for transcription.)

POVERTY ON THE LOWER EAST SIDE

An ancient and perhaps somewhat exaggerated rabbinic teaching claims that "if all the suffering and pain in the world were gathered [on one side of a scale] and poverty on the other, poverty would outweigh them all." The Jewish tradition, it is clear, has never celebrated poverty.

It was to escape destitution, as well as antisemitism, that millions of Jews fled eastern Europe for the "golden land" (*goldene medina*) of America. Yet once in this country, Jews, like other immigrants, learned that America did not automatically yield its "gold" to its newest arrivals. At the turn of the twentieth century, the average Jew arriving in America possessed nine dollars. Later, as Jews became America's most successful ethnic group, professionally and economically, many found it easy to joke about their parents' and grandparents' early poverty. Molly Picon, the Yiddish actress who later achieved prominence in the American theater, used to tell of how her mother raised ten children in a four-room apartment.

"How did she manage?" a friend asked.

"She took in boarders."

In fact, the poverty experienced by Jewish immigrants wasn't funny at all, but often grinding and embittering. A letter published in a 1908 issue of *The Forward* underscores just how stark life can become in a society without governmental welfare:

> One goes about with strong hands, one wants to sell them for a bit of bread, and no one wants to buy. . . . I get up at four in the morning to hunt a job through the newspaper. I have no money for carfare, so I go on foot, but by the time I get to the place there are hundreds before me. . . . Lately I've spent five cents a day on food, and the last two days I don't have even that. . . . I didn't come here for a fortune, but where is [the] bread?[1]

Most immigrants were more successful than this man in finding work, but they still toiled in circumstances that were oppressive. An 1885 article in Joseph Pulitzer's New York *World* reported that shirtmakers, generally young women, earned between $5.50 and $6.00 a week, and spent ten hours a day, usually six-and-a-half days a week, at a sewing machine. Unfortunately, the price for a clean bedroom in a "respectable" house with food was itself $5.00 a week. As the reporter goes on to note: "Washing at the lowest estimate is 50 cents per week, fire, a necessity in winter, 50 cents more. If lunch is not furnished [at work] that will be 60 cents per week, at the very least. And if a girl is obliged to ride to and from her work, that is 60 cents more for carfare."[2]

Many Jews, desperate to bring their families over from Russia, deprived themselves of basic necessities. In Anzia Yezierska's story "Brothers," the hero, a man named Moisheh, tries to save money to buy ship tickets for his mother and two brothers: "Moisheh the Schnorrer they call him. He washes himself his own shirts and sews together the holes from his socks to save a penny. He cooks himself his own meat once a week for Sabbath, and the rest of the time it's cabbage and potatoes or bread and herring. And the herring that he buys are the squashed and smashed ones from the bottom of the barrel. And the bread he gets is so old that he's got to break it with a hammer."[3]

A real-life character like this was Abe Sarnoff, father of David Sarnoff, the legendary founder of RCA. During his first years in America, Abe Sarnoff starved himself while working as a housepainter in order to send for his wife and children. By the time they arrived, he was

Hester Street, shown here in 1890, was one of the most famous streets of New York's Lower East Side. The Lower East Side was the first stop for most Jewish immigrants who came to America—the center of Jewish life in New York.

Above: *Many Jewish immigrants turned to factory work to make a living, and they were essential to the labor unions that fought to improve work conditions through demonstrations such as the one shown here.*

bedridden, and he remained so. David developed a successful newspaper route, sang in a synagogue choir, picked up an extra dollar or two singing at weddings and bar mitzvahs, and by age thirteen supported the entire family.

This grinding poverty is what inspired so many Jews to help develop labor unions, which eliminated some of the suffering. In 1900, Jewish garment workers created the International Ladies Garment Workers Union (ILGWU); the Union's later leader, David Dubinsky, became one of the most prominent union presidents in the United States. And a Jewish immigrant from London, Samuel Gompers, became the founding president of the American Federation of Labor (AFL) in 1886.

Perhaps the greatest impetus to Jewish involvement and support for labor unions was the 1911 Triangle Shirtwaist Factory fire in downtown Manhattan. Largely because the rear exit, a heavy iron door, had been locked by the factory owners, 146 workers, most of them Jewish women, died; it was a company policy to ensure that all employees left by one front exit, where they could be checked to make sure they had not pilfered anything.

The fire broke out in the factory's front, and with the back exit closed, the terrified employees had no escape route. Many jumped out of the high windows, and went crashing through the sheets that were being held to catch them. Rose Freedman, a member of my congregation in Los Angeles and the last survivor of the fire [she died in February 2001], said: "The executives with a couple of steps could have opened the door."

The extent of the tragedy—and the realization that it could have been largely averted had the building's owners not locked the exit—helped to bring about stricter fire-prevention regulations, worker's compensation, factory-building legislation, and increased support for unions. But whether they were in unions or not, Jews who worked so hard just to feed their families knew there was only one way to guarantee that their children led more comfortable lives than they had: education.

Right (inside flap): *Many lives lost in the tragic Triangle Shirtwaist Fire of 1911 could have been saved through safer workplace conditions. This event won great sympathy for the cause of labor unions and reformers.*

Poetry Inspired by Poverty

The pain such poverty inflicted is perhaps most powerfully expressed in poems by two great figures of American-Yiddish literature, Abraham Reisen (1876–1953) and Morris Rosenfeld (1862–1923). Reisen's "Family of Eight," rendered in rhyming English by the contemporary American-Jewish poet Marcia Falk, focuses on the anguish of a mother of six children, whose poverty imposes on her a life totally devoid of privacy.

Family of Eight

Only two beds
for a family of eight.
Where do they sleep
when the hour is late?

Three with the father
and three with the mother—
small feet and fingers
entwined with each other.

And when it comes time
to prepare for the night,
then Mama starts wishing
her death were in sight.

And what is the wonder
she'd rather be gone?
The grave's narrow too
but you lie there alone.[4]

Rosenfeld's poem "My Little Son" expresses the pain of a father who works from early morning till late at night to support a young son he fervently loves but almost never gets to see.

Mein Yingele (My Little Son)

I have a little boy, a fine little son.
When I see him, it seems to me that I own the whole world.
But I seldom see him, my little son, when he is awake.
I always meet him when he sleeps.
I only see him at night.
My work drives me out early and makes me come home late.
Strange to me is my own flesh and blood.
Strange to me is the look of my child.

When I come home shattered, wrapped up in darkness,
then my wife tells me how nicely our child plays,
how sweetly he chatters, how cleverly he asks:
"O Mother, good Mother, when will he bring me a penny my good, good father?"
I listen and yes, it must, yes, yes, it must happen!
Father love blazes up in me. My child, I must see him.
I must stand by his cot and see and hear and look.
A dream stirs his lips: "O where is Daddy?"
I kiss the little blue eyes.
They open, O child! They see me and quickly they close.
There stands your father, dearest, there you have a penny!
A dream stirs his lips: "O where is Daddy?"
I become sad and oppressed, bitterly I think,
when you finally wake, my child,
you won't find me anymore.[5]

Early twentieth-century Jewish immigrants clearly were concerned with the Jewish education of only their sons. In 1903 the 307 *cheders*, religious elementary schools on New York's Lower East Side, had a total enrollment of 8,616 boys and only 361 girls. As time went on, classes became more diverse. The picture below shows a Pittsburgh class in 1929.

Encouraging Education

Pullouts: While public schooling was important to all immigrants, it was emphasized particularly strongly in Jewish communities. Jewish parents saw free schooling as one of the key opportunities America offered them and their children, as these two posters (one from Cleveland in 1911 and the other from the 1930s) show.

(Yiddish text is the same as the English.)

A PASSION FOR EDUCATION

Harry Golden, author of the best-selling *Only in America* and a noted raconteur of Jewish immigrant life on the Lower East Side, recalled how immigrant women who couldn't speak English would go to a public library and "hold up the fingers of their hand to indicate the number of children they had. Then they would get a card, give it to each of their children, and say, 'Go, learn, read.'"[1]

Study has long been a sacred tradition in Judaism, going back to the Bible's insistence that "You shall teach it [the Torah] to your children" (Deuteronomy 6:7). The talmudic rabbis regarded this verse as the basis for legislating that parents were obligated to teach their children or hire others to do so. Among Jews, study was not only a commandment, it was, along with charity, a supreme commandment. This biblical law was translated two thousand years ago in ancient Israel into a system of universal education for boys, including free schooling for the poor.

In more modern times, many Jews transferred traditional Judaism's focus on religious studies into love for all study. In her memoir *The Promised Land* (1912), Mary Antin recalls how parents would bring children to their first day of school "as if it were an act of consecration." And while religious Jews spoke proudly of "my son, the *talmid chacham* (Talmud scholar)," less traditional but equally proud Jews now bragged of "my son, the doctor."

A large part of what made America a "golden land" for Jews was the availability of free education. In eastern Europe, a person born poor almost always died poor. True, a very basic Jewish education was provided free of charge to poor children, and the Jewish community frequently subsidized the education of advanced and exceptional *yeshiva* (seminary) students from impoverished homes. But that was the exception, not the norm. As for non-religious education, Russian schools imposed severe restrictions on how many Jewish students were accepted (the quota even had an official name, *numerus clausus*) and, in any case, the only Jewish students accepted were those whose families could pay full tuition. How inspiring it was for immigrants to arrive in a society in which it was possible for a poor person to go to elementary and high school, and even some colleges, free of charge.

Ample evidence indicates that immigrant Jews were willing in large numbers to "defer gratification" to keep their children in school for as long as possible. A 1907 letter from a teenage girl to *The Forward* asks for the editor's support of her decision to disobey her parents:

> Worthy Editor,
> . . . There are seven people in our family—parents and five children. I am the oldest child, a fourteen-year-old girl. We have been in the country two years and my father, who is a frail man, is the only one working to support the whole family. I go to school, where I do very well. But since times are hard now and my father only earned five dollars this week, I began to talk about giving up my studies and going to work in order to help my father as much as possible. But my mother didn't even want to hear of it. She wants me to continue my education. . . . Mother and Father work very hard and they want to keep me in school. I am writing to you without their knowledge and I beg you to tell me how to act.[2]

The editor's response was clearly supportive of the parents: Listen to your mother and stay in school.

One public school at which Jewish students eventually became a majority was New York City's prestigious Bronx High School of Science. Cultural historian Stephen Whitfield of Brandeis University notes that this school alone eventually produced more Nobel laureates in physics than Italy, France, or Japan ever had.[3] By 1900, twenty years after the beginning of the great Russian migration, the City College of New York had already been labeled with the unflattering nickname "the Jewish College of America." Jews referred to it with the more affectionate and accurate term "the poor man's Harvard."

Jewish students apparently gained a reputation for great intellectual abilities even among those who despised them. In 1936, Yale president James Angell, upon being informed of the large number of incoming Jewish students from the Connecticut cities surrounding Yale, joked, "If we could have an Armenian [style] massacre [against the Jews] confined to the New Haven district with occasional incursions into Bridgeport and Hartford, we might protect our Nordic stock almost completely [from Jewish competition]."[4]

Eugene Rostow, a child of eastern European Jewish immigrants and a student at Yale during Angell's presidency, wrote an article denouncing "ancient prejudice" at the university. Such denunciations, accompanied by decades of relentless Jewish pressure to modify the quota system, eventually paid off. Within three decades of his graduation, Rostow was hired by Yale as dean of its law school.

America offered Jews, as it offered all other immigrants (an offer that was not extended for much of American history to African Americans and Native Americans), what no other society had ever offered previously: free access to education from kindergarten through college. Although private universities openly and shamelessly discriminated against Jews (and didn't fully lower such barriers until the 1960s), public colleges operated on a merit system: if one had the grades, one was accepted.

The very openness of this society, matched by the intensity of the Jewish commitment to education, led to unprecedented Jewish professional accomplishments. Today there are three times as many Jews (in percentage terms) as non-Jews practicing medicine. In law, Jews are overrepresented by almost four times, in psychiatry by five times. And in Ivy League schools, Jewish students are represented more than five times their percentage in the population.[5]

American-Jewish Humor

The Jewish emphasis on education, and the professional success it helped ensure, became a staple of American-Jewish humor:

A joke: *A woman walking down the street with her two young boys encounters a stranger who asks their ages. "The doctor is four, the lawyer is two," the proud mother answers.*

A riddle: *"Why did the Jewish boy become a lawyer?"*

"He couldn't stand the sight of blood."

A notice in a Jewish newspaper: *"Mr. and Mrs. Marvin Rosenbloom are pleased to announce the birth of their son, Dr. Jonathan Rosenbloom."*

On the other hand, the underside of this obsession with education and professional success is the widespread shame over children who have not achieved white-collar status. As Jackie Mason, perhaps the most successful American-Jewish comic today, jokes:

"Did you ever see what happens if a Jew has a son who drives a truck? He's so embarrassed, he's hiding in Philadelphia! If you know any Jew, anywhere in the world, whose son drives a truck, say this:

'Does your son drive a truck?'

'Drive? I wouldn't say he drives. He sits in the truck, he doesn't drive it. I wouldn't say he drives it. How would it look, a truck is moving, there's nobody there? So, in case it goes out of control, he controls it. He's not driving it—he's controlling it. . . . That's it. He's a controller in the trucking business.'"[6]

Top: *At age 19, model Betty Joan Perske was "discov-ered" by movie director Howard Hawks, who signed her to a seven-year contract under the name Lauren Bacall.*

Bottom: *Erich Weiss, the son of Hungarian immigrant and Wisconsin rabbi Samuel Mayer Weiss, took the stage name Harry Houdini to pay homage to renowned French magician Jean Eugène Robert-Houdin.*

NAME CHANGES

An early twentieth-century Jewish joke tells of a man with a thick east European accent who goes into court and requests that his name be changed to Sullivan. The judge is puzzled. "Why just two months ago, I granted your request to change your name from Yankelovitch to Jones. Why do you want to change it again?"

"Because, your honor," the man responds, "every time I introduce myself as Jones, people ask me vhat my name vas before it vas Jones."

Jewish jokes (like all jokes) develop in response to significant events in the surrounding society. Jokes about name changes seemed to grow dramatically around the time that many American universities started asking questions such as the following in their applications: "If your family name has been changed, what was the name before the change?"

Columbia University's approach was slightly subtler. In 1919, at the direction of President Nicholas Murray Butler, the university began asking applicants to list their father's last name and birthplace. Within several years, such questions enabled Columbia's undergraduate division to cut its Jewish population by more than half and its medical school by far more; in the early 1920s Jewish enrollment at Columbia's College of Physicians and Surgeons was 50 percent; by 1940 it had been reduced to 6.4 percent. As Dr. William Rappleye, the medical school's dean, explained, "The [makeup of the] religious and racial group in medicine ought to be kept fairly parallel with the population makeup."[1]

The main reason so many Jews changed their names was to evade antisemitism. In the late 1940s, when Jews made up 6 percent of Los Angeles's population, they comprised 46 percent of those who went to court to obtain a new name.[2] Needless to say, antisemites weren't impressed by these Jewish efforts to Americanize. Henry Ford's antisemitic newspaper *The Dearborn Independent* viewed name-changing as another instance of Jewish deceptiveness, of Jews trying to smuggle their way into Gentile society.

The best-known name changes occurred among Jews who made their careers in Hollywood. Of course, antisemitism wasn't the only factor motivating such changes. Hollywood producer Samuel Goldfish simply wished to rid himself of a name that sounded somewhat foolish. The judge who granted his request to be known as Samuel Goldwyn declared: "A self-made man has the right to a self-made name."

However, many studio bosses, themselves Jews, believed that overtly Jewish names would "turn off" American Gentiles. Perhaps such names could be used in the more open atmosphere of the Broadway theater district (located in the center of New York City, the most Jewish city in the country), but they were not suitable for movies. In Ben Hecht and Charles MacArthur's play *The Front Page*, the governor's assistant is one Irving Pincus. In the 1940 cinematic remake of the play, *His Girl Friday*, the character is reborn as Joe Pettibone. Similarly, Clifford Odets named the fight promoter Roxie Gottlieb in his play *Golden Boy*, but in the 1939 film version of the play, the character is rechristened Roxie Lewis.

Hollywood bosses were certain that the American public would only accept typically American names in romantic leads. Thus, when Julius Garfinkle informed studio boss Jack Warner that he was taking the name Jules Garfield, he met with the objection: "What kind of name is Garfield, anyway? It doesn't sound American." The actor answered that it was the

Arthur Arshawsky

Israel Baline

Joyce Bauer

Nathan Birnbaum

Leo Jacob Cobb

Jacob Cohen

Issur Danielovich

Esther Friedman

Emmanuel Goldenberg

Avrom Hirsch Goldbogen

Theodosia Goodman

Melvyn Hesselberg

Isidor Iskowitch

Sonia Kalish

David Daniel Kominski

Allen Stewart Konigsberg

Joseph Levitch

Joan Molinsky

Eugene Orowitz

Alissa Rosenbaum

Bernard Schwartz

Jerome Silberman

Robert Zimmerman

name of an American president, James Garfield. When Warner responded that he should take the first name James instead of Jules, the actor protested. "But that's the president's name. You wouldn't name a goddamn actor Abraham Lincoln, would you?" A Warner executive broke in: "No, kid, we wouldn't, because Abe is a name that most people would say is Jewish and we wouldn't want people to get the wrong idea."[3] "John" was settled on as a first name, which is how Julius Garfinkle became John Garfield.

In recent years, as Jews have achieved far greater acceptance in American life, some Hollywood stars have come to believe that they can "make it" without disguising their Jewishness. Such has been the case with Barbra Streisand, Dustin Hoffman, Paul Simon, Art Garfunkel, Jeff Goldblum, and Ron Silver. Sometimes, there were even "reverse" name changes. Actress Tovah Feldshuh was raised as Terry Sue, Tovah being her seldom-used Hebrew name. But she retrieved it in the 1970s and her career was in no way harmed. Actor Richard Dreyfuss not only has kept his Jewish name, but also has been very public about his Jewish commitments: "In a sense, everything I do has to do with my being Jewish."

Perhaps the most surprising of Hollywood name changes suggests just how positive a Jewish image can be. Thus, Caryn Johnson, one of the most gifted African-American actresses and comedians, is rarely recognized under her born name. However, almost all Americans can identify her by her chosen name of Whoopi Goldberg. And David Wallace, son of the best-selling novelist Irving Wallace, reclaimed his family's original name, one that had been changed and shortened at Ellis Island. He has since published all his writings under the name David Wallechinsky.

The change in Jewish attitudes toward their names is well underscored by an incident my wife, Dvorah, witnessed. During the early 1980s, when she was working as editor, translator, and all-around assistant to Isaac Bashevis Singer, the Nobel Prize–winning novelist, she accompanied him to a lecture in Chautauqua, New York. A large reception was arranged at the home of a man named Livingston. During the reception, Livingston told Singer that his name had originally been Levtov, "good heart" in Hebrew. The family had changed the name to Leventhal, then to Livingston: "In those days, it would have put a big limitation on my father's practice if his name had sounded too Jewish."

When they left the dinner, Singer confided to Dvorah: "A few years ago, he would not have told me all this. He just would have said Livingston. But today, people are becoming proud again."

JEWS AND POPULAR CULTURE

What do "Take Me Out to the Ball Game," "Brother Can You Spare a Dime?," "Ol' Man River," "Oklahoma," and "Diamonds Are a Girl's Best Friend" have in common?

Each of these classic American songs was composed by a Jewish immigrant or child of an immigrant—respectively, Albert Von Tilzer (born Albert Gumm), E. Y. "Yip" Harburg, Jerome Kern and Oscar Hammerstein II, Richard Rodgers and Oscar Hammerstein II, and Jules Styne. Indeed, the involvement of Jews in popular music is so pronounced that to imagine twentieth-century America without this contribution is to imagine an American culture devoid of *Rhapsody in Blue* (George Gershwin), "Somewhere Over the Rainbow" (Harburg), *Guys and Dolls* (Frank Loesser), *West Side Story* (Stephen Sondheim and Leonard Bernstein), and *My Fair Lady* (Alan Jay Lerner and Frederick Loewe).

Most remarkably, the two most popular songs written in America about Easter and Christmas ("Easter Parade" and "I'm Dreaming of a White Christmas") were composed by Irving Berlin, the Russian-born son of a cantor. The composer of some 1,500 songs, Berlin wrote what many regard as America's second national anthem, "God Bless America." When he concluded that the song didn't work in the 1918 music revue for which he composed it, he dropped it, then brought it "out of storage" twenty years later when singer Kate Smith asked him for a patriotic ballad. So wide-ranging were Berlin's contributions that Jerome Kern claimed: "Irving Berlin has no place in American music, he *is* American music."

Equally, if not more striking is the Jewish contribution as movie moguls. A dozen men, almost all late nineteenth- and early twentieth-century immigrants from eastern Europe, developed the motion picture industry. They included Louis B. Mayer, the Warner brothers (Harry, Jack, Sam, and Albert), Samuel Goldwyn, and David O. Selznick. Indeed, the only non-Jew known as a mogul was Daryl F. Zanuck, who formed Twentieth Century Pictures with another Jewish film pioneer, Joe Schenk.

Louis B. Mayer, perhaps the most famous of the group, was born in Russia in 1885. The day he was granted citizenship he adopted the birthdate of July 4th as a tribute to his new homeland. Mayer formed Metro-Goldwyn-Mayer (MGM) in 1924, and over the following three decades, his studio produced many of the era's most successful, glossiest, and solidly middle-class pictures: *Mutiny on the Bounty*, *The Good Earth*, *The Human Comedy*, and the Marx brothers' *A Night at the Opera*. Mayer was known to place so many relatives on the company's payroll that people joked that "MGM" stood for "Mayer's *ganze mishpocha*" ("Mayer's whole family").

Generally, the moguls were uncomfortable with allowing Jewish themes to seep into film plots, fearing that Christian Americans would be uninterested or would oppose seeing such topics in films. Thus, *The Life of Emile Zola*, the highly acclaimed film that focuses in large part on the French novelist's valiant campaign on behalf of Captain Alfred Dreyfus, the French army officer who was falsely accused and convicted of treason because he was a Jew, tells the story of Dreyfus without mentioning the word "Jew." Indeed, it is difficult to figure out exactly why Dreyfus is being persecuted (hawk-eyed viewers will notice that in one scene, the audience is shown a list of French army officers; next to Dreyfus's name the word "Jew" is written). Similarly, Warner Brothers' 1939 *Confessions of a Nazi Spy*, a look into the work of Nazi supporters in the United States, speaks of Nazi calls for "racial unity," without acknowledging their antisemitic views or the antisemitism then raging in Germany.

Top: *The son of Russian-Jewish immigrants, George Gershwin composed many of the great American classics, including* Rhapsody in Blue *for the orchestra, the opera* Porgy and Bess, *and Broadway tunes like* "Someone to Watch Over Me."

Bottom: *In 1932, movie producer David O. Selznick, a first-generation American Jew, married Irene Mayer, the daughter of fellow Jewish movie mogul Louis B. Mayer. The marriage led to a professional union of the two moguls several years later.*

God Bless America

The ambivalence most of the moguls felt toward their Jewishness is best summarized by the story Ben Hecht tells about David O. Selznick, the famous producer of *Gone with the Wind*. Hecht, the highest-paid screenwriter of the 1930s, was himself an indifferent Jew until he learned of the Nazis' murderous campaign against European Jews. Suddenly energized and concerned, he approached Hollywood's leading producers, including Selznick, for help in publicizing the Holocaust.

Selznick's reply was firm: "I don't want to have anything to do with your cause for the simple reason that it's a Jewish political cause. And I am not interested in Jewish political problems. I am an American and not a Jew."

Knowing Selznick to be a gambler, Hecht proposed a wager. He would call any three people designated by Selznick and ask them whether they agreed that David Selznick was an American and not a Jew. If just one of them agreed, Hecht would leave Selznick alone; otherwise, Selznick would agree to help Hecht in his cause.

The first person Selznick instructed Hecht to call was Martin Quigley, publisher of the *Motion Picture Exhibitors' Herald*. "I'd say David Selznick was a Jew," Quigley answered. Nunnally Johnson, a screenwriter, "hemmed for a few minutes but finally offered the same reply." Selznick's last choice was Leland Hayward, an influential talent agent. "For God's sake," Hayward snapped, "what's the matter with David? He's a Jew and he knows it." A man of his word, Selznick agreed to cosponsor a fund-raising event with Hecht.[1]

The Jewish contributions to the world of American humor have been as marked as those to the music and film industries. Try to imagine American comedy without these twenty stars: Woody Allen, Jack Benny, Milton Berle, Fanny Brice, Mel Brooks, Lenny Bruce, George Burns, Sid Caesar, Billy Crystal, Rodney Dangerfield, Danny Kaye, Sam Levenson, Jerry Lewis, Groucho Marx, Jackie Mason, Zero Mostel, Joan Rivers, Mort Sahl, Phil Silvers, and Henny Youngman. Steve Allen, the late comedian and historian of American humor, estimated that 80 percent of the country's leading comics have been Jews.

In the first half of the twentieth century, many professions remained blocked to Jews. When my father came to the United States as a teenager in 1924, his dream was to be an engineer. But because engineering was a field closed to Jews prior to World War II, he became an accountant. The same sort of antisemitism prevailed in fields such as academia, banking, insurance, and the utilities. But popular culture was open to most minorities. And Jewish songwriters, movie moguls, and comedians entered it with enthusiasm, creativity, and imagination.

IRVING BERLIN, *the Jewish composer of dozens of American classics and a frequent entertainer of American troops stationed abroad during World War II, immigrated to America from Russia as a child.*

The National Songbook

"Between 1920 and 1965, American songwriters lifted the musical to a new level of excellence, as this partial list attests: *Oklahoma!, Annie Get Your Gun, Brigadoon, South Pacific, Gentlemen Prefer Blondes, Guys and Dolls, The King and I, Wonderful Town, The Pajama Game, My Fair Lady, The Most Happy Fella, Peter Pan, Camelot, Funny Girl, West Side Story, Carousel, Gypsy, Pal Joey, Paint Your Wagon, How to Succeed in Business Without Really Trying, A Funny Thing Happened on the Way to the Forum, Hello, Dolly!,* and *Fiddler on the Roof.*

"In high schools, in community theaters, and in revivals on Broadway, these musicals have been mounted again and again. The songs they introduced comprise a significant chunk of our national songbook: "I Got Rhythm," "I've Got a Crush on You," "Easter Parade," "Smoke Gets in Your Eyes," "Someone to Watch Over Me," "Oh, What a Beautiful Morning," "New York, New York," "There's No Business Like Show Business," "Almost Like Being in Love," "Some Enchanted Evening," "Diamonds Are a Girl's Best Friend," "Luck Be a Lady," "Hello, Young Lovers," "I Could Have Danced All Night," "Party's Over," "Maria," "Everything's Coming Up Roses," "If Ever I Would Leave You," "Hello, Dolly!," and "Sunrise, Sunset." Remarkably, Jewish-American composers and lyricists wrote every one of these songs as well as the shows in which they were featured."[2]

REFUGEES FROM HITLER AND DEATH CAMP SURVIVORS

The great Jewish migrations of the nineteenth and early twentieth centuries, both from Germany and eastern Europe, consisted of immigrants who, by and large, were uneducated and poor. The German-Jewish migration of the 1930s—the refugees from Hitler—broke half of this stereotype. These immigrants were poor, but uneducated they were not. Nineteen past and future Nobel laureates arrived in the United States during this eventful decade.

For the first time in American history, a large-scale migration occurred of people from solid middle- and upper-middle-class backgrounds, people who arrived not in search of economic opportunities but to save their lives. The German-Jewish migration did not begin in large numbers immediately upon Hitler's appointment as chancellor in 1933; it took several years until most German Jews realized how precarious their situation had become. Long known for their intense, often naive, loyalty to Germany, most of the country's 600,000 Jews were confident that Hitler's election was a temporary horror and that he would soon be ousted. Such optimism survived among many, even as Hitler organized a boycott of Jewish stores and ordered the removal of Jews from academic and government jobs as well as from other professions.

However, by 1935, when Hitler pushed through the Nuremberg Laws, withdrawing citizenship from Jews, more and more Jews began to understand that their history in Germany had come to an end. The problem was that it was difficult for Jews who wished to leave to find a place to go. As Chaim Weizmann, the Zionist leader, complained in 1936, "[For the Jews] the world is divided into places where they cannot live, and places into which they cannot enter."[1] Some German Jews sought refuge in Palestine, the historic Jewish homeland, which England controlled. But, anxious not to upset the Arab residents there, London severely restricted the number of Jews admitted to Palestine.

The eyes of most German Jews turned to the United States. But because of the regional bias of the quota restrictions imposed since 1924, German Jews could not immigrate there en masse. During the 1930s, however, Jewish refugees did make up the majority of people admitted under the German quota, a total of some 132,000.

It was difficult for many immigrants, some of whom were distinguished professionals in Germany, to adjust to their new, often much lower, status. The first job offered to Hans Morgenthau, later a distinguished political scientist at Harvard, was as an elevator operator. Kate Frankenthal, a prominent physician and author, sold ice cream on the streets of New York and hid her face when she recognized people she had previously met at lectures or medical conferences.[2]

On purely practical grounds, Hitler's extreme antisemitism proved a costly mistake. Edward Teller was forced out of the University of Göttingen and took a position at George Washington University, while Hans Bethe left the University of Tübingen for Cornell. Later, both won Nobel Prizes. Ultimately, Hitler drove out of Germany 43 percent of the country's academics, including Albert Einstein, the most prominent scientist of the age.

In 1933 when the Nazis came to power, Einstein, who was out of the country at the time, accepted a position at Princeton University's Institute for Advanced Study. In 1939, while in residence there, he received reports that German scientists had achieved atomic fission by

Top: *Albert Einstein, one of the greatest minds of all time, was a German Jew who was out of the country when the Nazis came to power. Einstein decided never to return.*

Bottom: *As the earliest of the refugees from Hitler began arriving in America in 1933, hundreds of thousands of New York Jews protested the oppression of the Jews in Germany under Hitler's new reign.*

splitting heavy uranium with a neutron bombardment. Worried about the implications of this research, Einstein drafted a letter to President Franklin D. Roosevelt that included Einstein's prophetic observation:

> In the course of the last four months it has been made probable . . . that it may become possible to set up nuclear chain reactions in a large mass of uranium, by which vast amounts of power . . . would be generated . . . . This new phenomenon [of atomic fission] would also lead to the construction of bombs, and it is conceivable . . . that extremely powerful bombs of a new type may thus be constructed.

The president summoned an aide, whom he told simply: "This requires action."[3]

Thus was set in motion the Advisory Committee on Uranium, which eventually turned into the Manhattan Project, under the direction of the American-born Jewish scientist J. Robert Oppenheimer. Historian Howard M. Sachar records that by 1943 Oppenheimer "assembled at Los Alamos and elsewhere perhaps the most outstanding scientific talent in America. Refugees formed the core of that talent—[Leo] Szilard, [Eugene] Wigner, Emilio Segrè . . . Edward Teller, Hans Bethe, Niels Bohr. . . . At Los Alamos, so many European Jews overflowed the Mesa that 'bad English' was the prevalent language. Only three of the center's seven divisions were directed by American-born scientists (two of these also were Jews)."[4]

The contributions of "Hitler's Refugees," as this 1930s migration often has been called, were not limited to the sciences. Other notable refugees included conductors Bruno Walter and Otto Klemperer, composer Arnold Schoenberg, film directors Otto Preminger and Billy Wilder, psychologists Bruno Bettelheim, Erik Erikson, and Erich Fromm, historian Hans Kohn, political scientist Hannah Arendt, sexologist Ruth Westheimer ("Dr. Ruth"), and a fifteen-year-old high school student, Henry Kissinger, who thirty-five years after his arrival became America's first foreign-born secretary of state.

When the Jews were expelled from Spain by Ferdinand and Isabella in 1492, many escaped to Turkey, where Sultan Beyazit II welcomed them warmly. "How can you call Ferdinand of Aragon a wise king," he was fond of asking, "the same Ferdinand who impoverished his own land and enriched ours?" Stanford historian David M. Kennedy has reached a similar conclusion in his assessment of contributions made by the 1930s refugees: "Hitler's . . . racialist policies bestowed a priceless intellectual endowment on the United States."[5] Indeed, the intellectual flight from Nazi-dominated Europe that began during the 1930s ensured that by the war's end, the world's intellectual leadership would shift, perhaps permanently, from Europe to the United States.

New Lives

Sociologist William Helmreich's *Against All Odds*, a meticulous study of the 140,000 survivors who immigrated to the United States in the 1940s and 1950s, reveals a striking variety of careers and activities among those who survived the Holocaust:

Harry Haft, a concentration camp survivor, became a professional boxer in the United States and fought against Rocky Marciano and other top professionally ranked fighters.

Abraham Foxman, saved by a Christian nanny in Poland who baptized him, today heads the Anti-Defamation League, American Jewry's leading defense organization. The League fights anti-semitism and all other such prejudices, and also promotes Jewish interests. Given Foxman's background, it is not surprising to learn that his mission in life is to expose and combat all Jew-haters and racists: "I don't think Jews have the luxury to look at any racist or antisemite as a kook."

Tom Lantos, a survivor of Nazi labor camps, has been a member of the House of Representatives from the San Francisco area for more than two decades. Shaped by his wartime experiences in Hungary, Lantos has long championed the persecuted, fighting battles on behalf of the Bahais in Iran, political dissidents in China, and children exploited in sweatshops. He also was the leader in the 1980s battle with the Soviet Union to uncover the fate of Raoul Wallenberg, the Swedish businessman and diplomat who saved over 20,000 Hungarian Jews—among them Lantos—in the last year of the war. Wallenberg was arrested by Russian troops in 1945 and apparently murdered in a Soviet prison in 1947. In an effort to bring attention to the case, Lantos pushed a special bill through Congress to make Wallenberg an honorary citizen. Winston Churchill is the only foreigner to have received this honor before Wallenberg.

U.S. Army Brigadier General Sidney Schachnow, a Holocaust survivor from Lithuania, where he spent his childhood years in a concentration camp, became a Green Beret (U.S. Army Special Forces) commander in Vietnam and later the commander of U.S. forces in Berlin.

Isabella Leitner, a novelist and memoirist, recalls her feelings on May 8, 1945, as she arrived in the United States on board the SS *Brand Whitlock*:

> Dr. Mengele, we are on our way to America, and we are going to forget every brutal German word you forced us to learn. We are going to learn a new language. We are going to ask for bread and milk in Shakespeare's tongue. We will learn how to live speaking English and forget how people die speaking German.

Left: *Jewish refugees and immigrants scoured the names of survivors found in liberated concentration camps to see whether friends and relatives still in Europe might be found.*

In the first years after the war, most of the Holocaust survivors who came to the United States remained silent about their experiences, sensing that the larger world of Americans, Jews and non-Jews alike, had no desire to hear about their sufferings. Many did not speak openly of their past even to their own children, fearing that to do so could be emotionally damaging. Others were less cautious. A close friend, whose mother was the sole survivor of an extended family of eighty-three, told me that his mother's graphic depictions of the murders of her relatives haunted his youth.

During those early years in the United States, the immigrants, almost all of whom arrived penniless, devoted themselves to raising their families and making a living. For many, this meant an enormous decline in status. Abe Foxman, leader of the Anti-Defamation League, remembers how his father, a respected journalist in Europe, had to take a job cleaning out the garage at Pechter's Bakery headquarters; later he ran a chicken farm in Toms River, New Jersey. David Brandt, a successful executive, recalls that his father, an engineer in prewar Lithuania, became a janitor in the United States:

> Only he never told us that. He said he worked in metals. One day after school I went down there and I was going to pick him up. Only he was not in front of the factory and I went inside looking for him and some people told me where he was. He was late, or maybe I was a little early, and I was shocked when I saw him washing that floor and that latrine. And that was the first time I had an inkling of what he did. I tried to move away, but he, he saw me. . . . We drove home and he cried . . . a terrible day.[6]

Unlike Foxman's and Brandt's fathers, many survivors had had little education, having spent their teenage years in concentration camps or in hiding. They too became blue-collar laborers or worked in jobs such as driving taxis or operating newsstands.

Survivors were as ambitious for their children as had been previous generations of Jewish immigrants, and many children of survivors achieved enormous professional success. In the series of more than a hundred in-depth interviews sociologist William Helmreich conducted with survivors, he was repeatedly struck by the unusually high number of survivors' children who had attended top universities. Frank Colb, for example, had three children, one of whom graduated from Harvard Law School, a second from the University of Pennsylvania, and the third graduated *summa cum laude* from Brown University.[7]

Two of the three most famous Jews in the U.S. today (the third is Senator Joseph Lieberman) were themselves victims of the Nazis: Henry Kissinger, the former Secretary of State, who fled Germany with his family in 1938, and Elie Wiesel, the Romanian-born survivor of Auschwitz who has done more than any other person to make the Holocaust known to the world. Wiesel's book *Night*, a recreation of his Holocaust experiences, is the first account many people read of the Nazi death camps.

Born in 1928, Wiesel was deported to Auschwitz at sixteen, and later to Buchenwald. There, he witnessed the death of his father, but managed to survive until the camp was liberated by the Allies. He titled his first book *Night* to under-

Saving the Children

Although many American Jews regret that they didn't do more to help victims and refugees of the Nazis, aid organizations were able to offer some assistance, particularly to children separated from parents during the Holocaust. The enclosed pamphlet raised awareness and funding for Jewish refugee children forced to leave parents behind in internment camps in France. A train carried these children out of France, through Spain, and into Portugal where they waited to flee the continent. Liesel Weil, who at the last minute replaced another sick child on the Portuguese liner *Mouzinho*, wore the enclosed tag so her American rescuers could identify her.

ELIE WIESEL, *winner of the Nobel Peace Prize, immigrated first to France and then to America after his liberation from the concentration camp Buchenwald.*

score the unrelenting darkness of the Holocaust experience. In 1986 Wiesel was awarded the Nobel Peace Prize. Although he is primarily known as a writer, the Nobel committee saw Wiesel's writings and public activities in making the Holocaust and its implications known—as well as his activities on behalf of causes such as Argentina's "disappeared" and the Kurdish and Cambodian refugees—as having helped make another genocide far less likely to occur to any group.

During a 1985 White House ceremony at which President Ronald Reagan presented him with a Congressional Gold Medal, Wiesel respectfully but firmly urged the president to cancel his proposed visit to Bitburg, a German military cemetery where forty-seven officers of the SS (the German division that carried out many Holocaust murders) were buried: "That place," he told Reagan, "is not your place. Your place is with the victims of the SS." Though visibly moved by Wiesel's remarks, the president did not cancel his visit to the cemetery.[8]

The "second generation" of Holocaust survivors, as an organization formed by children of Holocaust survivors calls itself, has shown intense interest in ensuring that the Holocaust retains a central place in Jewish consciousness. Thus, both survivors and their children have played dominant roles in the creation of over 150 Holocaust memorials throughout the United States. The most famous site is the U.S. Holocaust Memorial Museum, which opened in Washington, D.C., in 1993. CNN broadcast the dedication ceremony live throughout the world. As Elie Wiesel declared on that day, "Though the Holocaust was principally a Jewish tragedy, its implications are universal."[9]

One of the most powerful exhibits at the Holocaust Memorial Museum is that created by historian Yaffa Eliach, herself a survivor. Over several decades, Eliach assembled the history of Eishishok, the Lithuanian town where she was born and spent her early years. The floor-to-ceiling photographs Eliach collected of Eishishok are exhibited in a tower, and reflect the vitality of a Jewish community that had existed for nine hundred years, only to be destroyed by the Nazis and Lithuanian collaborators during two days of slaughter in September 1941. In other exhibits, visitors are confronted with massive piles of personal items such as suitcases, toothbrushes, and prayer shawls that guards confiscated from those who perished at Auschwitz.

A 1989 survey of American Jewry revealed that a sense of personal identification with the Holocaust ranked first as a marker of Jewish identity, ahead even of synagogue attendance on Rosh Hashana and Yom Kippur.[10] It is now estimated that survivors and their descendants make up 8 percent of America's Jews, but because so many of them are "fiercely committed to perpetuating the Jewishness for which they almost lost their lives," their influence on American-Jewish life has been disproportionate to their numbers.[11] Having arrived here half a century ago with the most devastating of physical and emotional wounds, Holocaust survivors have become an inspiration to many third- and fourth-generation American Jews.

Orthodox Revival

When World War II ended, there were still about 200,000 Jews in Hungary. Tens of thousands came to the United States, among them thousands of followers of the Satmar Rebbe, a Hasidic dynasty known for its rigid Orthodoxy, communal solidarity, and anti-Zionism; the movement's leader, Rabbi Joel Teitelbaum (1886–1979), believed that a Jewish state in Israel should be established only through the direct intervention of God, not through human efforts. Most of the movement's followers settled in Williamsburg, a neighborhood in Brooklyn, New York, where they helped create a vibrant, unexpected revival of ultra-Orthodox Judaism in the United States.

A greater influence on the broader American-Jewish community has been exerted by Lubavitch (also known as Chabad), a hasidic movement founded in Russia at the end of the eighteenth century. Its charismatic leader, the late Rabbi Menachem Mendel Schneersohn, known as the Lubavitcher Rebbe, came to the United States from Europe shortly after the beginning of World War II. He established a movement in Brooklyn with outposts in hundreds of American cities and throughout the world. Even following the rebbe's death in 1994, the community continued to grow and attract an unusual assortment of helpers. I once was amazed to hear actor Carroll O'Connor, famed for his TV role as Archie Bunker, making a radio pitch on behalf of the Los Angeles Chabad House.

Having grown up on New York's Lower East Side during the 1920s, my mother, who came from a traditionally observant Jewish home, told me that she was sure she was witnessing the final generation of Orthodoxy in American-Jewish life. For while she knew many Jews from Orthodox homes who were becoming nonobservant, she knew no Jews from nonobservant homes who were becoming Orthodox. But largely because of the Jews who migrated to the United States in the decade after the end of World War II, Orthodoxy has spread and become a more vital force in American-Jewish life than ever before.

"Let My People Go"
THE ARRIVAL OF THE RUSSIANS

Among many American Jews, the Holocaust provoked a deep sense of shame and guilt. It was widely felt that American Jews, fearing antisemitic repercussions, had not sufficiently pressured President Roosevelt during the 1930s to admit more Jewish refugees and later, during the war, to authorize the bombing of the railroad tracks leading to the Nazi death camps. Because of this legacy of guilt, when reports of Soviet antisemitism started to spread in the West during the 1960s and 1970s, many American Jews were determined not to repeat the inaction of their parents' generation. Of course, the Soviet Union, unlike the Nazis, was not seeking to physically annihilate the three million Jews who lived there, but only to destroy Judaism and Jewish identity. Thus, the government closed down synagogues, barred Jewish education (including the study of Hebrew), forbade emigration, and published antisemitic books, some of which accused Judaism of being a Nazi-like religion.

In response, student activists in New York founded the Student Struggle for Soviet Jewry in 1964, which was followed a few years later by the formation of the national Union of Councils for Soviet Jewry. In 1971 the largest Jewish organizations in the United States joined together to establish the National Conference on Soviet Jewry. The combined reach of these groups was extensive. When Soviet performers visited the United States during the late 1960s and throughout the 1970s and 1980s—whether they were a small string quartet or the world-famous Bolshoi Ballet—they invariably were greeted by Jewish picketers demanding rights for Soviet Jews.

At the same time, starting with Israel's inspiring success in the Six-Day War of 1967, an underground renewal of Jewish identity began to spread inside the Soviet Union. Throughout the USSR, small groups of Jews, aware that their activities could lead to imprisonment, started studying Hebrew and by 1969 began seeking permission to leave the Soviet Union.

At first when Soviet Jews received permission to leave Russia, most headed for Israel, but by the mid-1970s, emigrants who were seeking a higher level of national security and more favorable economic opportunities, as well as political freedom, started coming in large numbers to the United States. By 1990 the Brighton Beach section of Brooklyn housed over 45,000 Soviet Jews; ten years later, an estimated 200,000 Russian-speaking Jews lived there and in the surrounding South Brooklyn neighborhoods. Brighton Beach was widely known as "Little Odessa"; the spoken language both on the streets and in stores was Russian.

More than 300,000 Jews from the Former Soviet Union (FSU) had come to this country by 2000, and Jewish communities throughout the United States offered support to the new immigrants. From Altoona to Wichita to Sioux City, local Jewish federations and their family-service agencies assumed responsibility for the new immigrants' housing, medical-care costs, and children's needs such as summer camps. These groups also made extensive efforts to find employment for the Russian Jews.

Despite this generous reception, the move to America brought many of the immigrants heartbreak as well as joy. The Jews arriving from the Soviet Union were, like the refugees from 1930s Germany, a highly educated group. A 1981 survey revealed that 64 percent had received at least some higher education, and 25 percent were professionals. Historian

Top: *In the mid-1970s, protesters dressed in prison garb to demonstrate against the oppression of the Soviet Jews, who were prevented from practicing Judaism.*

Bottom: *Men dressed in prayer shawls marched around the Soviet Mission to the United Nations in New York in 1965 to protest the Soviet suppression of Jewish religious rights.*

Howard M. Sachar notes that "no other immigrant wave in American history . . . had quite approached this educational level."[1]

The immigrant scientists often were placed in academic positions, but the situation for non-fluent English-speaking lawyers, writers, social scientists, and musicians has been much more difficult. As one observer wryly noted: "There are few American job opportunities for classical accordion players."[2] Ironically, Soviet-born Jews do today make up a large percentage of the Philharmonic and other classical orchestras throughout the United States. An elevator man in my New York City apartment building served as the deputy director of an armaments factory in Ukraine, where he supervised over five thousand employees. Appreciative as he is of American freedom, this man finds painful the transformation from executive to elevator operator.

The transition in the United States has been difficult for other reasons as well. Steven Gold, a student of the Soviet-Jewish migration, observes that although Russian Jews share kinship ties "with the many American Jews whose roots are also in the precommunist Russian empire, their lives have been shaped by different forces: the Bolshevik revolution, the suffering and losses of World War II, and the unique conditions of life in a communist state, including, for Jews, discrimination and persecution."[3]

Like every generation of Jewish immigrants that preceded them, Jews of the Former Soviet Union are "zealous" about finding educational opportunities for their children. A study of the twelve largest immigrant groups in the New York City public school system revealed that children from the FSU ranked first in reading scores and second in math; indeed, their reading scores surpassed native-born students.[4] While this migration is too recent to be able to give a comprehensive report on the educational achievements of the second generation of Jews from the FSU, it is clear that the historic Jewish attraction to higher education is continuing among them.

In one significant regard, the Soviet-Jewish migration defies the pattern of earlier Jewish migrations from eastern Europe. The Jews who came over in the early twentieth century and after the Holocaust were, as a rule, more religiously observant and knowledgeable of tradition than the Jews then living in America. Because of their commitment to leading active Jewish lives, these earlier immigrations helped stem assimilation among American Jews. Soviet Jews are different in this regard. Unlike most American Jews, they have had almost no exposure to religious life or to a highly organized Jewish community.[5]

Russian Jews' commitments are generally limited to Jewish cultural and ethnic issues. And yet, American-Jewish history has shown that cultural and ethnic pride can sustain a Jewish community for perhaps two generations. By the third generation, non-practicing Jews generally weaken in their commitment to maintaining a Jewish identity and remaining involved in the Jewish community. Hence, two generations from now, will most Russian Jews be members of the American-Jewish community or "dropouts" from Jewish life? On this question, the jury is still out.

From Chess Prodigy to Rabbi

Leonid Feldman, a childhood chess prodigy, was the leading player in his age category in the province of Moldavia. It was the experience of being told that "a Feldman cannot represent Moldavia in a national tournament" that helped begin his search for his Jewish identity. This started the nonreligious Feldman (who at one time even taught state-sponsored courses on "scientific atheism") on a path that led to his incarceration in a Soviet prison and that culminated, twelve years later, with his rabbinic ordination at the Conservative movement's Jewish Theological Seminary in New York. Experiences like Rabbi Feldman's were repeated again and again throughout the Soviet Union.

LEONID FELDMAN

Theodore Roosevelt on Antisemitism

The creative way in which prominent, warmhearted Gentiles have shown their identification with Jews is reflected in the following story from President Theodore Roosevelt:

> While I was Police Commissioner [of New York City, in 1895], an antisemitic preacher from Berlin, Rector Ahlwardt, came over to New York to preach a crusade against the Jews. Many of the New York Jews were much excited and asked me to prevent him from speaking and not to give him police protection. This, I told them was impossible; and if possible would have been undesirable because it would have made him a martyr. The proper thing to do was to make him ridiculous. Accordingly, I detailed for his protection a Jew sergeant and a score or two of Jew policemen. He made his harangue against the Jews under the active protection of some forty policemen, every one of them a Jew.[1]

WHAT MADE THE "GOLDEN LAND" TRULY GOLDEN

"When a dog bites a man, that isn't news," declares the most famous of all newspaper sayings. "But when a man bites a dog, that is news." In discussing Jewish history, it is perhaps fair to say that when antisemitism happens, that isn't news; when philosemitism occurs, that is.

Philosemitism is, in fact, a term few readers might recognize; it means "affection for Jews." And while it would be naive to deny the significance of antisemitism in American-Jewish history—job discrimination long kept Jews out of fields such as engineering, academia, and banking, and most Americans opposed admitting more Jews fleeing for their lives from Hitler—what sets America off from so many of the other societies in which Jews have lived has been this country's openness to Jews, an openness that even predated the large-scale arrival of Jews in America.

Thus, at a time when Voltaire, the father of the French Enlightenment, inspired antisemitism in Europe (accusing the Jews, among other things, of having sacrificed non-Jews at their Temple in Jerusalem), President John Adams wrote to a friend: "In spite of Voltaire . . . I will insist that the Hebrews have done more to civilize men than any other nation."[2]

Moshe Genauer received his first big break in America. It occurred because his actions illustrated to a non-Jewish bank president that he was a decent and sincere man. As Blu Greenberg, the well-known Orthodox feminist and theologian, recalls:

> My grandfather Moshe Genauer came to America in 1905, at age twenty-six. The impetus was one more pogrom in the Ukraine. . . . He was a peddler [in Seattle, Washington] buying and selling used clothing. One day he walked four miles to the Queen Anne district (a wealthy neighborhood) to buy clothes from a man. He came back to his little room, laid the suits out on his bed, and found a diamond brooch in one of the pockets. So he turned around and walked all the way back to the house of the man who had sold him the suits.
>
> A woman answered the door. "I'd like to speak to your husband," my grandfather said. . . .
>
> "You can't bother my husband," the woman said. "You were here already. What do you want?"
>
> "I didn't buy a diamond from your husband," my grandfather replied. "I bought a suit."
>
> Her husband turned out to be the president of Rainier National Bank, and he rewarded my grandfather's honesty with an unlimited line of credit. This enabled my grandfather to bring over his wife, my uncle, and my father (then aged two), and later open a men's wholesale clothing business. And that is how I came to grow up in Seattle, the beautiful city of hills. The business became successful and supported six families the next generation.[3]

A year after Moshe Genauer's life-transforming encounter in Seattle, Viennese-born Felix Frankfurter, the only naturalized American ever to serve on the U.S. Supreme Court, graduated first in his 1906 class at Harvard Law School. In 1914, in what at the time seemed like a blow to antisemites, the Law School appointed Frankfurter to its faculty. Over the next few decades, Frankfurter waxed eloquent about the opportunities Harvard Law School offered

New Year's Greetings from a Land of Constant Promise

Pullout: New Year's greeting cards that featured traditional icons like the Star of David mixed with symbols of American freedom, industry, and opportunity, were very popular in American-Jewish communities of the early twentieth century. The Jewish appreciation for America as a uniquely welcoming land shows clearly in these cards, and has long encouraged new generations of Jews to seek a new and better life in this golden land. (See page 31 for translations.)

Jewish students, but in 1936, upon learning that eight Jewish editors on the *Harvard Law Review* had not received job offers, he wondered bitterly, "whether this school shouldn't tell Jewish students that they go through . . . at their own risk of ever having the opportunity of entering the best law offices."[4] The Law School waited a full quarter-century after Frankfurter's appointment to name another Jew to its faculty.

By the early 1970s, however, the barriers at Harvard and at all of America's elite universities had fallen completely. To cite one striking but not unique example: In 1973 Henry Rosovsky, who had fled Nazi Germany as a thirteen-year-old child, was appointed dean of Harvard's Faculty of Arts and Sciences, the university's second most powerful administrative post. When offered the deanship, Rosovsky, a committed Jew, told Harvard president Derek Bok that he would not give up his Jewish communal work and if that would in any way embarrass the university, Rosovsky would prefer not to be dean: "Bok couldn't have cared less." Six years later, in 1979, Rosovsky, carrying a Torah scroll, led a procession of faculty and students across Harvard yard, past the famed statue of John Harvard, to dedicate the new home of the Harvard-Radcliffe Hillel Society.[5]

What a difference four decades had made!

And what a difference another twenty-one years made, when in the first national election of the new millennium, Senator Joseph Lieberman of Connecticut, the most religiously committed Jew in Congress, was nominated as the Democratic vice presidential candidate, the first Jew ever named to a national party ticket. What was so striking about Lieberman's political career was the extent to which his religiosity was either a nonfactor or a positive one. Thus, when the Democratic convention nominated him for the Senate on a Saturday, he couldn't be present for his own nomination. Instead, he sent the convention a video, in which he explained to the delegates that he did not work on his Sabbath, but expressed his gratitude to the delegates for nominating him.

After such a publicized incident, his religiosity was well known to Connecticut voters, and it didn't seem to alienate many of them. In the Senate, his religious commitments did not hurt him either. Lieberman liked to tell the story of how a crucial Senate vote came up on a Friday night, and so he resolved to remain in the Senate while the matter was debated and voted upon; because he doesn't drive on the Sabbath, he intended to sleep on a cot in his office. When his then colleague Al Gore heard about this, he offered Lieberman accommodations at the nearby home of his parents.

Seventy-five years ago, job discrimination in American life was rife, newspapers routinely printed want ads with the words "Hebrews, no matter how qualified, need not apply," and hotels that catered to affluent Americans were "restricted." Now, as Lieberman's nomination has made apparent, there is no longer any position for which a Jew "need not apply." For America's six million Jews—a community overwhelmingly composed of immigrants and the children, grandchildren, and great grandchildren of immigrants—this seemed a remarkable way to start the new millennium.

HENRY KISSINGER *(on the left), pictured below at age 11 with his younger brother Walter, escaped the Nazi regime to become one of the most important statesmen in American history.*

Nobel Prize Winners

All five American Jews who have won Nobel prizes in Peace and in Literature have been immigrants: Henry Kissinger, the German-born former American Secretary of State, won the Peace Prize in 1973; Elie Wiesel, born in Sighet, Romania, won it in 1986. Saul Bellow, born in Canada to parents from Russia, won the prize for Literature in 1976, as did the Polish-born Isaac Bashevis Singer, the recorder of Jewish life and folklore in eastern Europe. Poet Joseph Brodsky, who grew up in Russia and immigrated to the United States as an adult, won the Nobel Prize for Literature in 1987.

Notes

The First Community
1. Jacob Rader Marcus, ed., *The Jew in the American World: A Source Book* (Detroit: Wayne State University Press, 1996), 29-30.
2. Ibid., 32-33.
3. Deborah Dash Moore, "[The Jews of] New York City," in *Jewish-American History and Culture: An Encyclopedia*, ed. Jack Fischel and Sanford Pinsker (New York: Garland Publishing, 1992), 458.
4. Richard B. Morris, "The Role of the Jews in the American Revolution in Historical Perspective," in *American Jewish History*, ed. Jeffrey Gurock (New York: Routledge, 1998), 1:53.
5. Ibid., 55.

The Arrival of the German Jews
1. Jacob Marcus, ed., *The Jew in the Medieval World: A Source Book, 315-1791* (Cincinnati: United American Hebrew Congregation, 1938), 167-169.
2. Howard M. Sachar, *A History of the Jews in America* (New York: Alfred A. Knopf, 1992), 41-42.
3. Barry Supple, "A Business Elite: German-Jewish Financiers in Nineteenth-Century New York," in *The American Jewish Experience*, ed. Jonathan Sarna (New York: Holmes and Meier, 1997), 100.

The Jews of Eastern Europe
1. Jack Fischel and Sanford Pinsker, eds. *Jewish-American History and Culture: An Encyclopedia* (New York: Garland Publishing, 1992), 270.
2. As paraphrased in Salo Baron, *The Russian Jew Under Tsars and Soviets* (New York: Macmillan, 1976), 49-50.
3. Arthur Hertzberg, *The Jews in America: Four Centuries of an Uneasy Encounter* (New York: Simon and Schuster, 1989), 13.
4. Milton Meltzer, *The Jews in America* (Philadelphia: Jewish Publication Society, 1985), 60.
5. Gerald Sorin, "Russian Immigration," in *Jewish-American History and Culture: An Encyclopedia*, ed. Jack Fischel and Sanford Pinsker (New York: Garland Publishing, 1992), 270-271.
6. Cited in Milton Meltzer, *A History of Jewish Life From Eastern Europe to America* (Northvale, New Jersey: Jason Aronson, 1996), 199-200.
7. Irving Howe, *World of Our Fathers* (New York: Harcourt Brace Jovanovich, 1976), 535.
8. Metzker, ed., foreword and notes by Harry Golden, *A Bintel Brief: Sixty Years of Letters from the Lower East Side to the* Jewish Daily Forward (New York: Doubleday, 1971), 24.
9. Cited in Meltzer, *A History of Jewish Life From Eastern Europe to America*, 212.
10. Cited in Henry L. Feingold, *Zion in America: The Jewish Experiences from Colonial Times to the Present* (New York: Twayne, 1974), 123.

German Jews v. Russian Jews
1. Ande Manners, *Poor Cousins* (New York: Coward, McCann and Geoghegan, 1972), 59.
2. Robert A. Rockaway, *Words of the Uprooted: Jewish Immigrants in Early Twentieth-Century America* (Ithaca, NY: Cornell University Press, 1998), 6.
3. Naomi Cohen, *Jacob H. Schiff: A Study in American Jewish Leadership* (Hanover, New Hampshire: Brandeis University Press/University Press of New England, 1999), 144-152.
4. Ibid., 136
5. Manners, 115.
6. Cited in Cohen, 109.

Poverty on the Lower East Side
1. Metzker, 76.
2. Cited in Milton Meltzer, *A History of Jewish Life From Eastern Europe to America*, 236.
3. Cited in Jonathan Sarna, ed., *The American Jewish Experience*

(New York: Holmes and Meier, 1986), 104.
4. "Family of Eight" by Abraham Reisen, translated from the Yiddish by Marcia Falk. Copyright © 1975 by Marcia Lee Falk. Used by permission of the translator.
5. Rosenfeld's poem is reprinted in Lionel Blue and Jonathan Magonet, *How to Get Up When Life Gets You Down* (London: Collins, 1988), 126-127.

A Passion for Education
1. Metzker, 66.
2. Metzker, 70-71.
3. Stephen Whitfield, *American Space, Jewish Time* (Hamden, Connecticut: Archon, 1992), 10.
4. Ibid., 9.
5. Nathan Glazer and Daniel Patrick Moynihan, *Beyond the Melting Pot*, 2nd edition revised (Cambridge, MA: M.I.T. Press, 1970), 157; Richard Reeves, *American Journey* (New York: Simon and Schuster, 1982), 280; Ernest van den Haag, *The Jewish Mystique*, rev. ed. (New York: Stein and Day, 1977), chapters 10 and 11.
6. Jackie Mason, *Jackie Mason's "The World According to Me!"* (New York: Simon and Schuster, 1987), 73.

Name Changes
1. Marcia Graham Synnott, "Anti-Semitism and American Universities," in *Anti-Semitism in American History*, ed. David Gerber (Urbana, IL: University of Illinois Press, 1987), 251-258.
2. Leonard Dinnerstein, *Anti-Semitism in America* (New York: Oxford University Press, 1994), 125.
3. Neal Gabler, *An Empire of the Their Own: How the Jews Invented Hollywood* (New York: Crown Publishers, 1988), 301.

Jews and Popular Culture
1. Ben Hecht, *A Child of the Century* (New York: Simon and Schuster, 1954), 539-545.
2. Jules Chametzky, John Felstiner, Hilene Flanzbaum, Kathryn Hellerstein, *Jewish American Literature* (New York: W. W. Norton, 2001), 961-962.

Refugees from Hitler and Death Camp Survivors
1. Joseph Telushkin, *Jewish Wisdom* (New York: William Morrow, 1994), 580.
2. Mark Anderson, ed., *Hitler's Exiles* (New York: The New Press, 1998), 6.
3. David M. Kennedy, *Freedom From Fear: The American People in Depression and War, 1929-1945* (New York: Oxford University Press, 1999), 660.
4. Sachar, 527.
5. Kennedy, 658.
6. William B. Helmreich, *Against All Odds: Holocaust Survivors and the Successful Lives They Made in America* (New York: Simon and Schuster, 1992), 141.
7. Ibid., 145-146.
8. Telushkin, 552-553.
9. From Wiesel's speech at the dedication ceremony.
10. Stephen J. Whitfield, *In Search of an American Jewish Culture* (Hanover, New Hampshire: Brandeis University Press, 1999), 186.
11. Edward Shapiro, *A Time for Healing: American Jewry Since World War II* (Baltimore: Johns Hopkins, 1992), 126.

The Arrival of the Russians
1. Sachar, 925.
2. Steven J. Gold, "Soviet Jews in the United States," in *American Jewish Year Book, 1994*, ed. David Singer (New York: The American Jewish Committee, 1994), 21.
3. Ibid, 3.
4. Ibid, 29.
5. Ibid, 3.

What Made the "Golden Land" Truly Golden
1. Cited in Allan Gould, ed., *What Did They Think of the Jews?* (Northvale, New Jersey: Jason Aronson, 1991), 285-286
2. Letter to Reverend Francis Van Der Kemp, February 16, 1809.

3. Myrna Katz Frommer and Harvey Frommer, *Growing Up Jewish in America: An Oral History* (New York: Harcourt, Brace & Co., 1995), 76.
4. Silberman, 96.
5. Ibid., 100-101.

Transcriptions

Page 4, George Washington Letter (English)
To the Hebrew Congregation in Newport Rhode Island.

Gentlemen,

While I receive, with much satisfaction, your Address replete with expressions of affection and esteem; I rejoice in the opportunity of assuring you, that I shall always retain a grateful remembrance of the cordial welcome I experienced in my visit to Newport, from all classes of Citizens.

The reflection on the days of difficulty and danger which are past is rendered the more sweet, from a consciousness that they are succeeded by days of uncommon prosperity and security. If we have wisdom to make the best use of the advantages with which we are now favored, we cannot fail, under the just administration of a good Government, to become a great and a happy people.

The Citizens of the United States of America have a right to applaud themselves for having given to mankind examples of an enlarged and liberal policy: a policy worthy of imitation. All possess alike liberty of conscience and immunities of citizenship. It is now no more that toleration is spoken of, as if it was by the indulgence of one class of people, that another enjoyed the exercise of their inherent natural rights. For happily [page 2]

the Government of the United States, which gives to bigotry no sanction, to persecution no assistance requires only that they who live under its protection should demean themselves as good citizens, in giving it on all occasions their effectual support.

It would be inconsistent with the frankness of my character not to avow that I am pleased with your favorable opinion of my Administration, and fervent wishes for my felicity. May the Children of the State of Abraham, who dwell in this land, continue to merit and enjoy the good will of the other Inhabitants; while every one shall sit in safety under his own vine and figtree, and there shall be none to make him afraid. May the father of all mercies scatter light and not darkness in our paths, and make us all in our several vocations useful here, and in his own due time and way everlastingly happy.

G. Washington

Page 6, Traveler's Prayer Book (title page in Hebrew, Yiddish, and German)
[title page]
Daily Prayer Book [*Tefilla Mikol Hashana*]. Small Offering for Travelers and Sea Farers to America (God Bless It). A Miniature Edition of Fine Beautiful Print. Fürth. In the year 5620 [1860]. Published by S.B. Gusdorfer. Printed by J. Sommer.
[handwritten inscription]
To my beloved
Small is my offering. / Let it not be compared to my love. / Please know that it comes from me: / a sign of love for thee / from Moses Margolioth. / 28 May 1875
[The other pages of this book contain prayers better suited to explanation than to direct translation. This extremely abbreviated version of the traditional *siddur* (prayer book) contains several of the prayers from the daily morning service, including the well-known "*Adon Olam*" (this prayer, like many others, is named after its opening words), the traditional blessings recited each morning, and the verse "*Sh'ma Yisrael*" ("Hear O Israel, the Lord is our God, the Lord is One").

Page 11, Theater Poster (in Yiddish, with the English words "Arch Street Theater" at top)
The gala event of this season in the Arch Street Theater
Thursday eve, the 22nd of March
The evening to honor
The young gifted comical actor
Mr Ludwig Satz
Who will appear for the first time in Philadelphia
In the great artistic role as
Feivel Holdak
In the "Russian Jew in America"
by Jacob Gordin
With the cooperation of
Ladies: Celia Adler, Esther Waxman, Mollie Picon and Lucy German
Gentlemen: David Baratz, Boris Rosenthal, Misha German, Moses Silberstein, Max Skurnik and Lazar Freed
Tickets are already available at the box office
At Colonial Coffee, 514 S. 5th St.
At Louis Schwartz's Hat Store, 932 West Girard St.

Page 13, Emma Lazarus's "The New Colossus" (English)
The New Colossus.

Not like the brazen giant of Greek fame
With conquering limbs astride from land to land;
Here at our sea-washed, sunset gates shall stand
A mighty woman with a torch, whose flame
Is the imprisoned lightning, and her name
Mother of Exiles. From her beacon-hand
Glows world-wide welcome; her mild eyes command
The air-bridged harbor that twin cities frame.

"Keep, ancient lands, your storied pomp!" cries she
With silent lips. "Give me your tired, your poor,
Your huddled masses yearning to breathe free,
The wretched refuse of your teeming shore.
Send these, the homeless, tempest-tost to me,
I lift my lamp beside the golden door!"

1883.
(Written in aid of Bartholdi Pedestal Fund.)

Page 21, "God Bless America" Lyrics (English)
God Bless America
Land that I love
Stand beside her
And guide her
Through the night with a light
From above
From the mountains
To the prairies
To the ocean
White with foam
God Bless America
My home sweet home.
Irving Berlin

Page 29, New Year's Greeting Card (mostly Yiddish, with Hebrew)
[Note: This card is based on the traditional Jewish blessing for 120 years of joyful life. This blessing is based on Gen. 6:3 (where God declares human life will not exceed 120 years).]

[central text]
Happy New Year Ship Ticket
Valid for 120 annual round trips on the stream of life.
May it be thy will, Lord our God and God of our fathers, that you should lead us toward peace and guide our footsteps toward peace in the journey of life for all our days. May you watch over us and rescue us from every enemy and ambush on the way and from all types of calamities which storm upon the world. And may you bless all our endeavors. [based on the Prayer for Travelers]
For He shall give his angels charge over thee, to keep thee in

all thy ways! [Ps. 91:1]
Every bearer of this free ticket has the right, alone or with the whole family, to make 120 times an annual trip.
Each round trip is from the New Year, when it is announced through the sound of the shofar [ram's horn]. Each passenger will receive free of charge for the whole trip life and peace, livelihood and sustenance, joy and mirth, redemption and salvation, and all that is good in great measure.
Each passenger can take with him as free baggage charity and good deeds and can perform during the life-long journey as many benevolent deeds as he wishes.
[signed] The Almighty Ruler of the ship of life, under the direction of the Creator
In addition to the above-mentioned free baggage, everyone can take with him all items necessary for joyful celebrations during the 120-year journey. For example: presents for Bar Mitzvahs, presents and things for the weddings of one's children and one's friends, namely gold, diamonds, and fine clothing from the wealthiest director on the ship, the Sustainer of Life.
[left border text, top to bottom]
A year that You should lead us with pride to our land [from the daily liturgy]
A year of life, peace, joy and mirth, and redemption
[right border text, bottom to top]
Blessed shall you be when you come in, and blessed shall you be when you go out [Deut. 28:6]
A year that You should bless our goings and comings
[bottom border text]
Sent by:
For:
[within top left symbol:] Golden Book of the Jewish National Fund
[within top right symbol:] Zion

Acknowledgments

I am particularly grateful to Ben Raker of becker&mayer! for his nuanced reading of *The Golden Land*, and for his perseverance and dedication to improving the book's contents and presentation. I also would like to thank Dale Cotton for contributing earlier work on this manuscript, Katie LeClercq for adding a beautiful design, Cindy Curren for coordinating production, and Adrienne Wiley for guiding the research of removable documents. As always, I am grateful to Toinette Lippe, my dear friend and editor at Bell Tower/Harmony, for her trademark dedication to every detail of this book, and to my close friend and extraordinarily capable agent, Richard Pine. I would also like to acknowledge David Szonyi for his careful reading of the manuscript and his numerous stylistic improvements. And finally, I would like to thank my beloved mother, Helen Telushkin, who, throughout my life, has entertained and inspired me with stories of her childhood on the Lower East Side and in Brooklyn, and who has so helped generate my own love of history.

Photo Credits

Key
AJHS: American Jewish Historical Society, Waltham, Massachusetts and New York, New York
CB: Corbis/Bettman
JTS: Courtesy of The Library of the Jewish Theological Seminary of America
LOC: Library of Congress
NYPL: New York Public Library, Milstein Division of U.S. History, Local History & Genealogy
USHMM: United States Holocaust Memorial Museum
YIVO: YIVO Institute for Jewish Research

Cover photo: Courtesy of the American Jewish Joint Distribution Committee. Front endsheet (Orchard Street, Looking South from Hester Street, 1898): Museum of the City of New York, The Byron Collection (5154). p. 2 Spanish Jews kneeling: CB. p. 3 Rabbi Aboab: JTS; Inquisition: CB. p. 4 Washington letter: Courtesy of Touro Synagogue; View of New Amsterdam, 1650–53 (background pp. 4–5): Original in the Government Archives, The Hague. Facsimile in the Museum of the City of New York, The J. Clarence Davies Collection. p. 5 Bank note: AJHS; Salomon portrait: United States George Washington Bicentennial Commission. p. 6 Prayer book: JTS; German emigrants: LOC; Peddler cart (background pp. 6–7): AJHS. p. 7 Seligman: AJHS. p. 8 Pogrom victims: YIVO. p. 9 Ellis Island dock: William Williams Collection, NYPL; Outside flap image ("After the Pogrom," 1905 oil on canvas by Maurycy Minkowski): Tel Aviv Museum of Art. p. 10 Saluting flag: YIVO; Orphans: Courtesy of the Statue of Liberty National Monument. p. 11 Grand Theater, exterior, 1903: Museum of the City of New York, The Byron Collection; Theater posters: AJHS. p. 12 Backstreet synagogue: LOC; Booklet: JTS. p. 13 Lazarus portrait: LOC; Poem: AJHS. p. 14 Hester Street: NYPL, Lewis W. Hine Collection. p. 15 Strikers: Brown Brothers; Fire: New-York Historical Society (54044). p. 16 Schoolchildren: AJHS; Cleveland Education poster: National Museum of American Jewish History; WPA poster: Work Projects Administration Poster Collection (LOC). p. 17 New York school: Brown Brothers. p. 18 Bacall: CB; Houdini: CB. p. 20: Gershwin: CB; Selznick and Mayer: CB. p. 21: Lyrics to "God Bless America" used by permission of The God Bless America Fund; Berlin at piano: CB. p. 22 Einstein: LOC; Protesters (p. 22 and background pp. 22–23): CB. p. 24 Refugee list: CB; Pamphlet and nametag: Liesel Weil Appel, courtesy of USHMM Photo Archives. p. 25 Wiesel: CB. p. 26 Protesters (both images): CB. p. 27 Feldman: Temple of Emanu-El of Greater Miami/Roslyn Dickens. p. 28 Roosevelt: CB. p. 29: New Year's card: HUC Skirball Cultural Center, Museum Collection, photography by John Reed Forsman; Kissingers: CB. Back endsheet (Orchard Street, New York City, 1933): CB.